WHAT
ARE
PEOPLE
SKILLS,
ANYWAY?

WHAT
ARE
PEOPLE
SKILLS,
ANYWAY?

SUSAN K. MACIAK

A 21st century how-to guide for improving human relations

To order additional copies of this book, contact:
Xlibris Corporation
1-888-795-4274
www.Xlibris.com
Orders@Xlibris.com
109817

Contents

Acknowledgements 9

Overview..11

Part 1

Chapter 1   People Skills Matter Now More than Ever...15

Chapter 2   Guidelines for Getting Along..................22

Chapter 3   What Are People Skills, Anyway? 28

Chapter 4   Our Actions Carry the Most Clout.........34

Chapter 5   Do You Recognize Good People Persons? ...39

Chapter 6   Communication: The Core of Human
             Relations 48

Chapter 7   Sacred Cs of Communication 62

Chapter 8   21st Century Communication:
             Less Can Be More.................................83

Chapter 9   The Lost Art of Listening.......................88

Chapter 10   Six Listening Styles for Six Situations....92

Part II

Chapter 11 Sharpen Your People Skills...................108

Chapter 12 Build Bonds from the Beginning..........123

Chapter 13 Rebuild Broken Trust.........................130

Chapter 14 Mind Your Manners . . . Monitor
Your Character....................................138

Chapter 15 ABCs of School and Office
Interpersonal Skills 147

Chapter 16 People Skills for Supervisors and
Managers 156

Chapter 17 Good People Skills = Good
Customer Service 161

Chapter 18 Use People Skills to Play the
Networking Game................................171

Chapter 19 Ace an Interview . . . with
Perfect People Skills 179

Chapter 20 People Problems and
Practical Solutions 188

What Are People Skills, Anyway? This book is more than a self-marketing manual for job seekers. It's a summary of everything that makes people personable and relationships work. It's a bible for building trust . . . a compass for compassion . . . a handbook for human relations.

Acknowledgements

What Are People Skills, Anyway? The manuscript for this book reached the publishing stage only through my husband John's capacity to cope with strange patterns of concentration, midnight floods of new ideas, and other creative quirks that made life difficult for him.

I'm grateful for my editor Veronica Hughes, who found me on Facebook and came back into my life to motivate me to set a deadline and finish this book.

Thanks, also, to the many hundreds of career coaching clients, workshop participants, high school and college students who inspired me to study employability issues and led me to investigate, uncover and understand secrets surrounding the mystery of people skills.

Overview

Before reading this book, take a moment to answer two crucial questions:

- *Do you list "people skills" as one of your strengths on your résumé?*
- *Can you explain what you mean when you claim to have good people skills?*

Nine out of 10 job-seekers promise, at least on paper, that they would come to a new career equipped with people-ability. Most candidates claim to possess people skills, though, only because they know that many job descriptions require them as prerequisites. The truth is that very few adults can actually define these elusive traits.

When pressed for answers in job interviews, the typical applicant can only answer vaguely with something like: "I'm good with people." A handful of others go beyond this basic notion, expanding with a little more detail. Their responses might include "I work well with customers" or "I cooperate with my colleagues." Yet, ambiguity reigns. A lot of adults can't really describe their ability to get along with other people.

That failure leads to the common, but baffling, question: ***What Are People Skills, Anyway?*** A manual for marketing yourself and a human relations handbook, this book covers what everyone needs to know to be a real people person in the 21st century. It's an easy-to-follow, how-to guide for building better relationships.

What Are People Skills, Anyway? This book is a summary of everything that makes people personable. It's a bible for building trust. It's a compass for compassion. It's a guide for using people skills to hone harmony at home and create cultures that are conducive to more productive companies. This self-improvement manuscript shows readers how to build trust and better handle people.

"If you don't learn how to build relationships, you'll limit your success," says contemporary author Sheryl Richardson. Her words are especially true in the 21st century. Making connections with others is the key to getting ahead in today's world. Whether it's through networking, volunteering or joining community groups, assembling a support base is a smart thing to do. There's never been a time in history when people need people more than they do now.

Some individuals seem to be born with skills that allow them to connect easily with others. Those people are neighborhood leaders who can chair cohesive committees, create cooperative teams and get along with everyone without any assistance. Most of us need help. Anyone who wants to be more successful in their day-to-day relationships will benefit by reading **What Are People Skills, Anyway?** Since early times, both the famous and the obscure have proclaimed the power of people skills. Nuggets of this notion lie in each of these examples:

No act of kindness, however small, is ever wasted.
—Aesop

Five things constitute perfect virtue; gravity, generosity, sincerity, earnestness, kindness.
—Confucius

The royal road to a man's heart is to talk to him about the things he treasures most.
—Dale Carnegie

Constant kindness can accomplish much. As the sun makes ice melt, kindness causes misunderstanding, mistrust and hostility to evaporate.
—Albert Schweitzer

Perhaps the most important thing we ever give each other is our attention.
—Rachel Naomi Remen

The most basic of all human needs is the need to understand and be understood.
—Ralph Nichols

There are two things people want more than sex and money . . . recognition and praise.
—Mary Kay Ash

An owner's manual for people-ability, this book provides valuable insights on interpersonal interaction from communications to customer service, from credibility to trust, honesty and ethics. ***What Are People Skills, Anyway?*** could be the key to your future.

Chapter 1

People Skills Matter Now More than Ever

People-ability carries careers, companies, companions, communities.

Anyone who's scanned the classified ad section recently knows that *people skills* are in demand. These sought-after traits top nearly every list of job qualifications. Career opportunities ranging from clerk to chemist call for candidates with good people skills. Whether help-wanted ads or job postings appear online, in a newspaper, on the radio, or on TV—most seem to scream for employees equipped with ability to work well with other people. In eras of increased competition for fewer positions, people-ability can determine the difference between being hired or not hired.

For most of us, it's simply a matter of understanding what people skills really are, making sure we have some and being able to articulate those skills in interviews. Even 16-year-olds working in fast-food restaurants are rated on their people skills today. Your uncle's boss or brother-in-law's supervisor may have sent him out of town for a three-day seminar on the subject. Your cousin probably became top salesperson at her company because she was trained well in dealing with customers or clients. You may get that promotion you've always wanted once you've polished your people skills.

When political candidates aren't elected, they're often accused of lacking people-ability. The pundits tell us that winners received more votes because they played better to the crowd or appeared to be more personable or caring. It doesn't matter what kind of campaign politicians plan. They can debate on TV, rub shoulders in malls, go door to door or speak to the masses in stadiums or arenas. The extent of their people skills still predicts their success or failure at the polls. In the same way, your people-ability could be the key to your career success.

The grapevine (wherever it grows) gives credit to anyone with enough savvy to get along with others. The new school superintendent, the city manager and the pastor at the Presbyterian Church are all expected to arrive on the job with perfect people skills. Five-year-olds need such talents to take on kindergarten, and 65-and-older folks fare better at local senior centers with good interpersonal skills. There are different degrees of people-ability. On a wide continuum, skills range from almost-none to advanced levels of expertise.

Examples:

1. A preschooler concedes that his friend found the fire truck first and lets it go. At the same time, his grandfather, who recently retired to Florida, stubbornly refuses to meet any of his new neighbors. "What for?" he grumbles.

2. One young couple brings a bottle of wine to show appreciation for a dinner invitation while

another pair doesn't show up at all—and doesn't bother to call to cancel. The difference in each case: *people skills.*

Times change and so do traditions in etiquette, tact and other social skills. Some conventions still stand. Other social norms have disappeared, been modified or changed altogether. Behind us now are many old customs once expected of everyone, including:

- Gentlemen tipping their hats to ladies
- Mandatory head covers for women in church and other public places
- Chatting with neighbors across the fence or on the front porch
- Wearing black for a whole year to mourn the death of a loved one
- Using formal titles like Mr., Mrs. and Miss when addressing people

Wearing Easter bonnets may be old hat, but some social customs have stayed the course. According to advice columnists, forgetting to send thank you notes for gifts continues to be a sign of poor people skills—as well as an unforgivable sin. Although the thought remains the same, the method of delivering appreciation may be different in the 21st century. Expressing gratitude through email, in most cases, can be just as acceptable as sending handwritten notes, once standard form. Formal occasions, though, such as weddings or graduations, still require personal thank you notes, hand-written in ink. We no longer bow from the waist when introduced to someone or expect children to be seen and not heard. Curtsies and other courting traditions may have come to an end, but common courtesies still matter in current times.

Society still depends on some civility. Despite other relaxed rules of the day, the ability to get along with others remains indispensible. In fact, there's a growing need to co-exist cohesively in crowded cities, on fast-paced highways and bumper-to-bumper byways. We live in a seemingly smaller universe, where interpersonal skills matter more than ever. Our leaders need to practice good people skills to ensure good international relations. We live in times when their smiles, smirks or frowns flash around the world instantly via satellite TV. Business people, sales representatives and anyone else who makes a living by working with people, must be able to get along with them. To survive and thrive in today's global marketplace takes above average expertise. Whatever we do affects folks from nearly every country and culture, no matter which language is spoken.

Wherever a company does business, employees with exceptional interpersonal skills attract and keep customers. Phone etiquette, email manners and texting tact all need to be heeded. Americans may have trouble understanding the accent of the person at the help desk in India, but appreciate the polite, patient friendliness practiced by those faraway folks. Personal finesse and willingness to please customers can be understood in any accent. Comments like, "Please get yourself a cup of hot coffee while we install your new software together" has a huge impact when the person on the other end of the phone provides service across two continents.

People skills make a dizzying difference in our fast-paced technological world. Take the expression *high tech-high touch*, for example. That short phrase, framed to define our mechanical modern life, sheds light on an important current issue: *Amidst ever more sophisticated technology, people still long for the personal touch.* We've all complained about today's techno-troublemakers, or griped about the grip machines have on our lives. New inventions have replaced real people in so many places, including:

- impersonal email contacts
- automated phone messages
- self-help information sites
- and other services delivered mechanically without a real person behind the lines.

Humans still crave contact with other humans. The time is right to renew our focus on fostering good human relations and put personal touches back into offices, schools, businesses and communities.

> *Social problems—from rising suicide rates to school shootings or mass murders in public places—beg us to examine interpersonal skills in today's society.*

A litany of social problems—from rising suicide rates to school shootings or mass murders in public places—beg us to revisit interpersonal relations in 21st century society. Almost daily, shocking incidents provoke us to ask, "What can we do to get along better with one another?" We all know we have to do something to keep the world from spinning out of control, yet only a few so far realize where to begin.

According to sociologists, preachers and police officers, crime rates would decrease if all people connected better with each other. That's why churches send missionaries to inner cities and pastors offer programs to help people solve their personal problems. It's also the reason police stations across the country try to keep neighborhood cops on the beat.

People skills, or lack of them, affect every aspect of living. Increasing episodes of violence illustrate the effect of severely broken relationships at their most basic level—in the family. Almost every day in our country a wife or mother goes missing, only to be found dead within miles of her home. Children are neglected or abused in every county of all 50 states. Kids gun down their parents, wives hire assassins for their husbands and school bullies beat up on anyone who annoys them. Even family pets take the brunt of lost civility in many households. When road rage kills innocent passengers on our streets, or schoolchildren die on sidewalks for no reason, it's clear that we need to review the role of people skills and their place in today's world. Manners, social standards and consideration for others cry out for a comeback.

Although people skills are more important than ever, many of us have a long way to go to become good people persons. While some individuals learn early in life how to interact successfully with friends, family and neighbors, others must be taught. Once parents, teachers, politicians and community leaders take a stand, younger generations will learn from example. Schools don't offer courses in people skills, and colleges don't grant degrees in them. However, anyone can become a good people person at any age by making up their minds to understand, practice and build better interpersonal relationships.

Remember

- People skills or lack of them affect every aspect of life.
- People skills can make or break careers, companies, marriages, families.
- Poor people skills can cause calamities ranging from business failures to mass murders.
- Good people skills can be learned at any age through example and with effort.
- Good people skills are especially important in today's global economy.

Rehearse. Think about a recent situation where someone's lack of people skill irked you or hurt you. Rewrite the same scenario the way you would have liked to see it happen.

Chapter 2

Guidelines for Getting Along

Old and new advice applies to successful human relations.

Guidelines for getting along with others are not new. Rules for interpersonal interaction appeared as early as ancient times. Old etchings on rocks and stone walls portray humans hunting together in harmony or preparing food together in caves. Good people skills are at least as old as the Old Testament. How to treat others was clearly outlined in the 10 commandments. The Golden Rule provides the best example of people-ability: *Do unto others as you would have them do unto you.* That theory of fair play remains one of the best-known bits of ancient wisdom. The Golden Rule reminds us that we should treat others as we would like others to treat us. People who aspire to live closely to this principle handle others with care. They're not only considerate of their friends, relatives or members of their own ethnic groups, but they also show respect to people of all backgrounds. The Golden Rule is voiced in various ways in the philosophies of ancient Babylon, Egypt, Persia, India, Greece, Judea and China. Some scholars believe that Confucius first called this concept "the golden rule." Many religions, including Hinduism, Buddhism, Taoism, Zoroastrianism and nearly all of the world's other major faiths expect their followers to abide by this sage standard of behavior.

In their natural wisdom, Native Americans came to the same conclusion as inhabitants of far-away lands. The words of caution to "walk in another's moccasins" before judging them is their version of the Golden Rule. Native Americans advise their peers to put themselves in another person's place before saying or doing anything derogatory. In other words, ask yourself, "How would I want to be treated in the same situation?"

Karma carries a similar message in other cultures. Believers maintain that everything you do *to,* or *for,* another individual eventually returns to you with equal impact. Good is rewarded with good. Bad comes back to bite you. If you show respect, others will give regard to you. If you attack another person, someone else will eventually ambush you. You get what you give.

> *No matter how far back sacred books go, they all spread similar messages.*

No matter how far back they may go—the Bible, the Koran, the Talmud, the scripture of Hinduism—each spread parallel messages on how to live peacefully with other human beings. Standards for interpersonal behavior can also be found in tomes as early as the *Analects* and *Five Classics,* containing the sayings of Confucius. Firmly rooted in most contemporary cultures are principles of valuing the lives, liberty and property of others.

"Before you embark on a journey of revenge, dig two graves," Confucius warned long ago. In today's words, he would say: "You're digging your own grave when you try to get even with anyone." His wise words are still relevant. The high price of revenge is covered nightly on television by crime-solvers like Nancy Grace, Paula Zahn, Vinnie Politan and Jane Velez-Mitchell. Our daily news is packed with headlines about humans treating others harshly, cruelly or unfairly, often to get even with them. Screenplays written for *CSI, Law and Order, Criminal Minds* and scores of other detective dramas prove daily through their plots and characters that the cost of humans harming other humans can be high. Only mutual respect makes it possible for people to live together harmoniously.

> ***Mutual respect forms the foundation for good people skills.***

In the 1930s, Dale Carnegie revolutionized the concept of valuing others in his well-known book, *How to Win Friends and Influence People.* His best-seller spread the interpersonal skills message around the world. In his preface, Carnegie explains how he stumbled on the need to help people get along better with one another. After hosting hundreds of popular public speaking seminars, he reveals, he gradually realized something significant from listening to his audiences. He heard clearly that many folks sorely need "training in the fine art of getting along with other people." That insight changed his presentations—and the course of Carnegie's career.

He crammed his workshops, along with his book, with advice on interpersonal relations. His new goal was to "help ordinary folks succeed in everyday business and social contacts." His book, still printed in dozens of languages, circles the world from west to east, north to south. It can be found in almost any library and bookstore yet today. Carnegie's unique tips for interpersonal relations include such gems as, "Get the attention, time and cooperation of even the most sought-after people in America by becoming genuinely interested in them."

Good people skills—or ability to get along with others—will never go out of style. Mutual respect, which forms the foundation for interpersonal relations, is needed now more than ever in our new world economy. The difference between an international corporation's success and failure in the 21st century depends on its people—and how they treat their customers. If employees are rude, uninterested or unwilling to provide consumers with pleasant assistance, their contacts will find friendlier folks elsewhere to sell them products or services. Customers can take their business almost anywhere in the world. All it requires is the click of computer keys, a few key words and a quick Google search to find the same item with better service and often lower cost, also.

Despite their location, buyers can go online to select goods from different suppliers or multiple shops and stores around the world. Locally, competition sprawls on every corner. Employees who demonstrate good people skills ensure that their customers keep coming back. Those who don't could soon be out of work. High quality merchandise counts, but not as much as the people who deliver products and services to the public.

Good human relations are more important than ever. Interpersonal interaction matters. Relationships matter in the marketplace, in marriages and family life and in community life. History verifies that it's been a struggle for mankind to maintain love and respect for one another as all great books and lasting religions of the world advocate.

Current events compel us to revisit wise counsel of past generations, along with paying attention to our people skills. The need for better human relations has reached critical mass. When a raised finger or a dirty look causes a drive-by shooting on the expressway, it's time to reexamine our collective people skills. When stupid remarks or social blunders cost people their jobs—or their lives—it's essential to take action. People skills are more important than ever.

Remember

- Building good relationships with others is not new to the 21st century.

- All major religions and cultures have stressed practicing good people skills.
- Good interpersonal skills matter in any relationship, including marriage and families.

Chapter 3

What Are People Skills, Anyway?

Hundreds of traits, habits and attitudes lead to good people skills.

HELP WANTED: *Only candidates with good people skills need apply.* You've surely seen this common clause in help-wanted ads posted on the Internet or printed in your local paper. If you've been out job-hunting lately, you know that almost every employer expects you to possess something called *people skills.* You think you know what they are and you're pretty sure you have some . . . but do you? What are people skills, anyway?

If you agree that people skills involve *getting along with others,* you're on the right track. But if your next pay raise or promotion depends on proving your expertise in interpersonal matters, what would you say? Where would you start? A quick Google search for ideas might give you a few hints, but not the whole story. Revisiting your college notes won't tell you much either. There aren't many books in the library, CDs, DVDs, or iPad apps that tear into this topic. Everyone seems to assume that people are born with people-ability. They're not.

Your one-page résumé may provide a peek at your interpersonal ability with words like *pleasant, friendly* and *easy-going.* Unfortunately, the same adjectives appear over and over again in vitas, résumés and cover letters. If such vague and over-used words are the only clues, your people-ability will remain a mystery to human resource professionals. Often, when interviewers ask candidates to describe their people skills, many job candidates can only stutter, "Well, I'm *helpful* . . . or I'm *nice.*" Such concepts are so trite that they're often completely ignored by résumé readers. After a while, worn out expressions lose all meaning. They're just empty words.

Job candidates who describe themselves with such generalities risk sending the wrong message, hindering rather than helping themselves. Using tired adjectives, such as *outgoing* or *friendly,* can sabotage a job candidate rather than suggest significant people-ability. Short taglines like these are wide open to interpretation. "Is this person going to spend all their time socializing or telling jokes?" an interviewer may wonder. A good résumé writer paints a picture of her best interpersonal behavior, using action verbs followed with specific details. Which is better?

Candidate A claims to be:
- Pleasant, considerate, nice
- Friendly, easy-going, energetic

Candidate B illustrates her people skills by explaining that she:
- Treats all customers, clients and fellow employees with respect
- Considers the feelings of fellow workers in all office interactions

- Suggests compromises to settle disagreements among co-workers
- Recognizes other people's skills, abilities and high-quality work

It's plain to see which person actually possesses people skills. When a candidate can provide concrete examples rather than relying on meaningless clichés, she proves her point. Which candidate would you hire?

You may agree that strong interpersonal skills matter in many ways, but still ponder: *What are people skills, anyway?* Simply stated, *people skills* are good traits, habits and attitudes that allow someone to get along well with others. People-ability combines hundreds of personal characteristics that make it possible to navigate through society successfully. Often called interpersonal skills, these important attributes define us. They paint a picture of each one of us for others to see.

Good people skills walk us through life easily, leaving a trail of good will behind us. Our people-ability determines whether or not we'd fit into a team, a company, an agency or an organization of any kind. Poor people-ability is analyzed on psychiatrists' couches across the country. Without the ability to get along with others, most of us are in trouble. Lacking people skills makes many individuals more than likely to lose friends, be fired from jobs or become involved in family feuds. Our traits, habits and attitudes—good or bad, right or wrong—determine our status in life.

Custodians need people skills as much as company presidents do. If a janitor shrugs his shoulders when a customer asks a question, as if to say "How should I know?" his company's image suffers. If corporate executives hide away in high offices and avoid interacting with employees or customers, commitment to their company declines. When poor people skills cross all levels of an entity or organization, its days in business become numbered. Everyone is at risk of losing their livelihoods.

> *Hundreds of good habits, traits and attitudes make someone a real people person.*

Personality traits such as charming, cheerful or charismatic make up a slim slice of the people-ability pie. Hundreds of good habits, traits and attitudes go into making someone a real people person. A positive attitude can be an asset. A genuine interest in others gives us an edge. Good manners put us at an advantage. People in the habit of smiling, greeting everyone they meet, or making those around them feel comfortable have a head start. Those who consistently carry out desirable social conventions also lead the pack. Actions like responding to invitations, saying *please* and *thank you*, apologizing for wrongdoing or admitting mistakes make anyone a better people person. Such qualities can be pivotal in everything from landing a job to leveraging a successful organization or launching a successful marriage.

Not everyone knows which social skills are most significant or how to develop them. For example, a well-qualified accountant and recent immigrant to the United States couldn't understand why she was called for many interviews but never hired. Her credentials were stellar, her experience in Europe remarkable and her English better than many native-born U.S. citizens, yet she could not advance beyond a first interview. Although she listed interpersonal skills as an important asset on her résumé, she failed to smile, shake hands or keep good eye contact during a series of mock interviews conducted at a job placement center.

This woman needed to learn and practice primary people skills expected for job interviews. She's not alone. Many homegrown candidates have lost jobs or failed to find new positions due to their poor people skills. Some never follow up after an interview with a phone call or write a thank-you note. Others don't realize that bad-mouthing former employers shows poor people-ability. Many have no idea that being personable or sharing a sense of humor can make a difference in who's hired and who's not, or who's promoted and who's not.

Good people skills matter in many life journeys. Individuals with interpersonal assets are more likely to make marriages work, raise considerate kids and create caring communities. Employees with good people skills can help build a business, an agency or organization. People who strive to improve their interpersonal skills can change relationships between themselves and their partners, between parents and their children, and among groups gathered together as co-workers, committee members, volunteers, parishioners, planners or party-goers. Learning and applying a wide array of interpersonal strategies can be a win-win game for everyone involved.

Rehearse

1. What are some habits, attitudes and personality traits that make a person a *naturally* good people person?
2. Which people-ability qualities would be easy to acquire with practice?

Chapter 4

Our Actions Carry the Most Clout

Our people-ability is on display in how we act toward others.

Attitude is important. Carefully choosing words is essential, but it's our behavior or actions that clearly convey our people-ability or lack of it. Sure, individuals with upbeat attitudes score more people points than complainers or naysayers do. Positive people attract more fans or followers than negative folks. Good word choice, tact and good judgment go a long way, too.

Discretion, according to the old adage, is a big part of valor. However, people-ability is best demonstrated in the way we behave toward others. Our actions carry the most clout.

What you do or don't do says the most about your people-ability. If you know enough to punctuate talk with action, you're ready for the big leagues. Actions like calling to RSVP, responding to requests or following through on promises will help you gain stature as a people person. If a neighbor is always cheerful and friendly, but never does anything to help anyone else, he's not going to be known as a people person. Only action added to attitude will take him to that level. Those who are most willing to go out of their way for others become the best *people-persons* in the eyes of their peers.

Whether it's stopping to encourage fellow employees, giving a ride to a stranded friend, bringing back coffee for a colleague or taking time to listen to your kids, you're acting like a people person. A leader who makes it a point to call on everyone at the table, rather than letting a few dominate meeting discussions, demonstrates people-ability. Friends or co-workers who consistently offer to help others behave like good people persons. Their actions speak louder than their achievements or honors.

Mastering people-ability is like developing any other skill—swimming, bike riding, reading, writing, tennis, cooking or computer programming. Interpersonal skills can be learned, but they also need to be practiced and perfected. To join the ranks of people persons all you need to do is learn the basics and practice them to reach effective levels of expertise. While it may sound like a lot of work, acquiring people skills always pays off. Adequate supplies of people-ability can help people achieve goals as diverse as:

- Opening new doors to the job market
- Closing deals or wrapping up sales
- Influencing others in important matters
- Getting the cooperation you need
- Bringing people to the polls to vote for you
- Gaining admiration and respect in your community

Polishing your people skills can bring pleasure to your personal life and pride to your professional pursuits.

Ignoring advice for improving interpersonal interaction is likely to invite emptiness, loneliness and frustration. People with good interpersonal skills are more likely to:

- Attract reliable friends
- Enhance every relationship
- Build functional families and communities
- Breed success in business and professional advancement

Poor people skills, on the other hand, cause resentment between co-workers, dig deep chasms among friends, and divide and destroy families. Shoddy social skills break down relationships, create conflict and establish enemies. Why would anyone resist perfecting their people skills? There are so many advantages for people who can get along well with others.

Unfortunately, too many of us erroneously believe that we are already armed with plenty of interpersonal ability. Most of us are fooling ourselves. Simply co-existing with other humans does not qualify us as good people persons. Reading about interpersonal skills isn't enough either. Only putting new insights into action will work. People-ability depends on how we behave in everyday situations—at home, at school, at work or in the community. Retaining what we read, taking lessons or learning about a subject is never enough. It's our actions that count.

Examples:

A. A high school student has excellent understanding of algebra, for instance, but can't use his knowledge to solve problems. He continually fails math tests. In that case, he does not have higher math skills. He is not what you'd call a *math person.* He only knows the principles behind the math, not how to practice or use those concepts.

B. A supervisor may think she knows a lot about human behavior. She may even have studied psychology, acing all her courses. She can understand the concept of people skills, but if she can't get along with her staff, she does not practice what she knows. She's not using her knowledge to build better interpersonal relations.

Anyone whose career, whose marriage, whose family or friends rely on interpersonal relations (*and they all do*) needs to assess their daily encounters with others. People-ability, or lack of it, will be most evident in how we act, how we react, how we approach others and how we work together or play together in groups.

Each potential people person should ask himself or herself: *Am I acting like someone who really cares about other people? Do I consider the best interests of others in everything I do? Am I kind to others? Am I caring?* If your answers take more than a second to surface, you may need a self-improvement plan. Give yourself at least three new action assignments every day. Make a short list first thing each morning. For example, remind yourself to:

1. Send a note to a sick friend.
2. Call a discouraged relative.
3. Open a door for someone.

Add three new actions every day and you could accumulate 156 more people skills every year. Start building your stash now!

Remember

- Personality traits, habits and attitudes form people skills.
- People-ability depends on how we act toward other people.
- Good people skills matter in all walks of life.

Rehearse. Send a thank-you note to a friend or co-worker who helped you recently or send a "thinking of you" card to someone you know who is struggling.

Chapter 5

Do You Recognize Good People Persons?

All good people persons are students of human nature.

How do you know who's well-equipped and who's not with interpersonal ability? Do you know good people skills when you see them? Are you aware of your own mistakes when your people-ability is less than perfect? Do you recognize good people persons in your every day encounters? There are several small signs that mark anyone who is likely to get along well with others. You can be fairly sure you meet a good people person when he or she:

- Smiles at others during the course of the day
- Takes time to listen to comments, concerns and questions
- Follows up on promises made, responsibilities assigned or actions agreed on
- Acknowledges special events—or tragedies—in someone else's life
- Offers assistance when help is needed
- Treats everyone with equal respect, no matter their station in life

People-ability requires much more of us than just being present where other humans congregate. Because we tend to be around others doesn't mean we practice effective human relations. In other words, people-ability is not the same as sociability. A social butterfly may flit from place to place, be seen everywhere, know everyone in town, but still lack people skills.

A people person is not necessarily a popular person. Introverts and extroverts can be equally capable of caring. From either end of the personality spectrum, shy or social, people-ability is possible. Popularity is often based on *extrinsic* values—looking attractive, wearing name-brand clothing, keeping up with trendy hairstyles or driving expensive cars. People-ability stems from *intrinsic* values, such as respecting others and treating everyone with care and compassion.

People persons enjoy others for their differences, rather than expecting everyone to be just like them. They avoid joining cliques, taking sides or turning away from anyone who is not in their inner circle. Outward appearances such as attire, facial expressions, posture or demeanor can add important interpersonal dimensions to relationships, but it's the inner self that best predicts people-ability. To paraphrase a recent political quotation: You can't put makeup on a monkey and expect it to be a people person. It takes more than powder and gloss.

Behavior—what we do or don't do—determines our degree of people-ability. Everything from how quickly we answer phone calls to how we greet people in person makes a difference. How we word emails and what we post on social networks gives clues about our ability to get along with others. All our actions have implications. Letting a phone ring too many times before picking it up, for example, shows disrespect to callers. Expressing anger in emails by capitalizing all letters, insults recipients. Berating people or institutions on Twitter or Facebook offends almost everyone in a network of friends. Bad-mouthing others makes the perpetrator look worse than the scapegoat. Ask yourself before acting: *How will my actions be interpreted by others?*

Example:

A supervisor needs to tell a subordinate to dress more professionally at work. She would be totally out of line to address an issue like this while standing next to that person while he/she sits at a desk on the job. The best approach might be to schedule an out-of-the-office meeting. Getting together over coffee at a quiet café makes a better setting. Rather than beginning the conversation with something like, "Your appearance is all wrong for work . . ." the supervisor relies on good people skills. She starts with, "To help you advance in your career, I'd like to suggest that you pay more attention to the way most people in our office dress." Worded that way, the other person understands why it's in their best interest to dress differently for work.

Your actions, or body language, are especially important when you're tackling tough topics. If you sit, where you sit and how you sit in the company of others sends subtle messages about your interpersonal expertise. A person who wants to intimidate someone else, for example, often stands while the other person sits. Her position is purposely manipulated. Her action is calculated to overpower someone else by looking down at them instead of eye to eye.

Executives often remain seated behind their desks during unpleasant conversations or complaint sessions. Putting distance (or an object like a desk) between them keeps the disgruntled worker a little more subdued. On the other hand, therapists often sit right in the circle during support groups. Their willingness to place themselves at the same level as their clients breaks barriers between themselves and persons with problems. Comments flow more freely when people feel equal. The most effective leaders demonstrate their understanding of human nature in everything they do. It's natural for others to want respect in any relationship.

If you want to develop your people potential, you need to practice good interpersonal skills seven days a week, 24 hours a day, no matter what your surroundings or circumstances may be. You can't behave gallantly at work, but come home and go on a rampage. You can't snub the person next to you on the bus or growl at the toll-taker on the expressway, then expect to put on the charm once you get to work. Sooner or later, you'll look like a phony if you act like one. Your behavior has to be consistent. Otherwise, you might slip up somewhere.

Practicing people-ability in one place and not another can cause conflict you can't hide. You must consider the comfort and well-being of everyone to maintain the aura of a good people person. If you're the first one at monthly staff meetings, but arrive at home two hours late for dinner every night, your people skills need polishing. When you tell your teenager you'll attend his music concert—then forget to go, your people priorities must improve.

Unfortunately, spouses often forget to be kind and caring after years of marriage. Some act like Mr. Nice or Miss Sunshine to the rest of the world, while being rude, even downright nasty, to each other. A few partners go as far as to call each other names, or tell one another to "Drop dead!" or "Get out of my way!" While most couples keep their poor people skills to reasonable levels at home, their people-ability is still out of sync.

Problems start with small infractions like forgetting birthdays or anniversaries, grumbling when asked for help or using each other's personal possessions without permission. Each of these examples sounds harmless. Too many careless actions, though, lead to breaches that break down relationships. To save a marriage, couples are often asked to start a diary of their daily actions, describing how their behaviors affect their partner. Both parties are instructed to leave space between each entry to write in later what they should have said or done. Their notes provide them with an improvement plan for putting new ideas into practice.

You can memorize a book of etiquette, but if you don't put your knowledge into practice, you won't correct mistakes in your interpersonal relations. Learning and doing are two separate things. You need to do both to become a better people person. A surgeon who graduates from medical school with all As, but can't perform tonsillectomies or appendectomies successfully, is not a good doctor. Likewise, someone who studies people skills, then fails to put them into action, is not a good people person.

A good people person turns every truth about the human condition into a trait to be used in getting along with others. For example, look at this fact of life from basic psychology: *Everyone wants to feel important.* It's a concept worth knowing that only means what is says when it's practiced.

> **Example:** When children misbehave, most adults know that they are trying to seek attention. Why? Everyone from birth to death has a need to be noticed. All humans want to feel important. We all need *to matter* to someone else. So children who don't feel noticed or don't believe they matter to anyone often act out in misbehavior.
>
> Many kids who started out in life as troublemakers have turned into fine citizens because some adult with good people skills noticed them. Maybe a teacher or a coach noticed a special gift in that child and encouraged him to develop it. Once the child

started to feel important—as a football player, a musician, a writer, an artist or whatever—his need for attention was fulfilled. His behavior improved.

Most adults know and apply at least minimal interpersonal skill based on their own needs and their observation of human behavior. Most understand basic human needs. Consider a few simple examples of how you may already use people skills in your interactions with others:

A. You know that shouting at others usually upsets them, so you speak in a normal tone of voice when talking to everyone.
B. You understand that getting too close to people makes them uncomfortable, so you allow everyone enough space.
C. You realize from your own experience how painful disappointment can be, so you comfort others when their plans have been dashed.

Being a good people person requires revisiting, reviewing and sharpening your interpersonal skills regularly. You'll have to practice applying people principles the same way you practiced multiplying in math until it becomes second nature. Becoming a better people person is a lifetime pursuit. If you're not able to get along with certain individuals or can't seem to communicate with someone—whether at home, at school, in the workplace or anywhere else—it's time to brush up on your basic people skills.

Recognize

Yes or No? Circle Y for Yes, N for No, depending on how well each statement below describes people-ability (Yes) or lack of it (No).

1. Y N   Your spouse barks orders at you. You bristle and bark back.
2. Y N   You keep working on your project while a child describes an exciting adventure.
3. Y N   Co-workers ask for advice, but you say you're too busy to talk.
4. Y N   You're getting sick and tired of celebrating office birthdays.
5. Y N   You don't believe in going to office parties or socializing with fellow workers.
6. Y N   You look away when you meet strangers on the street.
7. Y N   You constantly find yourself raising your voice when giving orders.
8. Y N   If you can't make a meeting, you just skip it and hope no one will miss you.
9. Y N   You know it's not nice to look away when talking, but your eyes still wander.
10. Y N   You don't like funerals, so you never attend one.

KEY: N, N, N, N, N, N, N, N, N, N

Rehearse. Make a list of the people skills you observe in others every day. Next to each skill, explain how you will put it into practice.

Example:

Good people skills observed	How I will practice these good people skills
Look everyone in the eye.	*Make eye contact with everyone I pass on the street.*

Chapter 6

Communication: The Core of Human Relations

There are at least three elements to most communication.

All relationships start the same way. They begin with some form of communication. In every human encounter, there's an exchange of expression, thoughts or ideas. What many people miss, though, is that communication goes beyond words. Some experts believe there are at least three elements to every example of communication:

1. **VERBAL:** What we say
2. **NON-VERBAL:** How we look and how we act when we say it
3. **EMOTIONAL:** How our voice sounds when we say it

Most forms of communication involve both verbal and non-verbal language. Emotions also play an integral role. Messages can vary according to how communicators use each of these three elements. For example, parishioners hear a sermon differently when delivered by their pastor in a quiet monotone than they do when the message is belted out with fire and ferocity, punctuated with the priest's pumping fists. To understand more clearly how these three elements work together, take a closer look at each of these different aspects of communications and how each affects others.

1. Verbal Communication

Think of verbal communication as three Vs: *Voice, Vocabulary* and *Volume.* Each plays a part in practicing good people skills. Vocabulary, of course, is choice of words (simple or multi-syllabic, specific or general, descriptive or dull, etc.). Voice covers the tone or temperament of your words (friendly or hostile, casual or calculated, sweet or sarcastic). Volume, of course, refers to how softly or loudly you talk, or how much noise your voice makes.

Your vocabulary starts building at birth. As soon as you uttered your first coo, you began to build a verbal dictionary. As your word list grew, your parents probably encouraged you to try a variety of synonyms for sounds such as mama (mommy, mom, mother). They also advised you to avoid certain words. You learned quickly that saying things, like "Shut up" or "I hate you," would get you in trouble. *Why?* You may have wondered. Expressions like those are unfriendly, your parents probably explained. Mom and dad may have also warned you, "Words like that are bad." The child who learns early in life that words can hurt people gets off to a good start in developing people skills. If words like *stupid, crazy* or *fat* are considered to be off limit or out of bounds, a child (*or an adult*) is less likely to insult someone with the wrong choice of words.

Volume is the second V of verbal communication. Families teach their children at early ages to control the range of their voices. A father reminds his son to use his *inside* voice, rather than shouting across the dinner table in his *outside* voice. His outside voice, according to dad, is reserved for yelling to friends on a football field or playing hide-and-seek in the back yard. The boy begins to practice good people skills as he learns to lower his volume in certain social situations. The same parent may advise him to speak up or speak clearly when talking to adults.

Our tone takes on a life of its own.

The third V of verbal communication is voice tone. When we're not careful, our tone can take on a life of its own. If her tone sounds shrill, a woman becomes a shrew. If it's soft, she's considered caring, loving or sweet. If she never changes the tone of her voice, though, she's easily written off as ineffective, uninteresting, and unimportant. In relating to others, regulating tone of voice is as important as regulating temperature. If your voice comes across as too cold, it freezes out others. If it sounds hot under the collar, it makes people sweat. Some moderation in voice tone makes most messages better to hear and absorb. Adding a dollop of drama to the voice can also work miracles. Political speeches, sales presentations and stage shows are a few examples of situations where inflection, even exaggeration, can turn a trivial monologue into a masterpiece.

2. Nonverbal Communication

Nonverbal communication refers to messages sent by your body. Your posture or stance, your position (seated or standing, side-by-side or face-to-face) or your proximity or nearness to others are examples. Everyone sends unspoken messages with their body's movements. Arms, legs, trunk, head, neck, hands, feet—all tell a tale, along with our spoken words. Unvoiced sentiments sometimes say more than verbalized messages. Body language often *speaks louder than words.*

One person wrings his hands to show frustration or desperation. Another one paces while presenting a program, revealing self-doubt or impatience. Facial expressions and hand gestures give away more secrets than fair-weather friends often do. All body movements affect the quality of interpersonal communication. If you insist that you're not nervous, but your body shakes all over, your body language is more likely to be telling the truth. Start crying at mid-sentence when bringing bad news and recipients know immediately how devastating the situation is. What they see trumps what they hear. It makes no difference which words you use. What you do while you're talking to someone says as much or more than what you actually say to them. What messages do these actions convey?

- A co-worker taps his foot while discussing an upcoming project.

- A groom looks over his bride's shoulder during the entire wedding dance.
- A coach pats a basketball player on the back after scoring a three-pointer.

According to students of body language, every facial expression, every leg movement, every arm or hand gesture is interpreted by others at least 10 seconds before they absorb your words. Wearing a frown notes that you're not happy, even if you say you are. Raising an eyebrow shows your surprise or disbelief, despite your efforts to remain neutral. A speaker with open arms appears to embrace his audience. On the other hand, a presenter who holds his hands behind his back nonverbally reveals to his audience that he is closed or not open to other ideas or opinions. If he's hiding his limbs, he's likely trying to disguise something about himself. He may not want listeners to know how unprepared he is. Whenever our hands are tucked away someplace, our words lose some of their worth. It's human nature to be suspicious of people who appear to be concealing something.

Using arm and hand gestures mean so much in public speaking that orators are advised to amplify gestures, holding each motion longer than they would in ordinary conversations. Many well-known speakers become scholars of non-verbal language. Since an audience reads body language faster than they can process the words they hear, the best speakers prepare by practicing their movements to coordinate with their comments.

Non-verbal clues carry weight in every walk of life. A mate who continues to read text messages while a spouse is asking questions always gets in trouble. A young boy who can't look his neighbor in the eye because he just broke the neighbor's window gives himself away through his body language. A little girl who continually twists strands of her hair tells observers that she's anxious or uncomfortable. As any detective knows, a suspect who clams up or fidgets too much automatically arouses suspicion. Nonverbal clues interpreted in interrogation rooms have solved more than a few crimes.

The ultimate message in both verbal and nonverbal language might be saying and doing nothing at all. Some experts say that stone-faced silence could be the fourth component to communication. No communication—or the act of not expressing thoughts or moving muscles—can be extremely powerful. Silence itself sometimes speaks volumes. Avoiding someone or giving them the proverbial cold shoulder quite often makes a stronger point than any words would. Silence sometimes is more effective than shouting or screaming. It can say more than folded arms, frowns or looks of disapproval delivered in frightening phrases.

Example:
A partner forgets an anniversary or another important occasion. The loved one responds by saying nothing—absolutely nothing—all evening. It may take a while, but the offender eventually realizes what the other person is saying: "You

hurt me beyond words by not remembering this special event."

Body language alone often passes on plenty. The patrol guard at school crossings can stop traffic with a raised hand. A mother relies on a certain look to bring her brood back into line. A smile is often enough to ignite a relationship or a romance.

Silence can be an effective strategy, but it can also be deadly. If you must resort to using no verbal or non-verbal language, you need to know *when* and *when not* to apply this form of communication to send a message. It might work for parents who have said all they can say to their children without results. After telling their youngsters to go to bed eight or nine times, silence sometimes stuns kids into compliance.

In most cases, failure to communicate causes confusion, misunderstanding and mistrust. Chronic communication problems can occur when words are not exchanged. Common in marriage or relationship problems, one partner quits talking altogether. In silence, resentments often grow bigger than in discussion. Some arguments are actually more productive than complete silence. Not saying anything at all is especially dangerous in the workplace.

Missing explanations or lapses in accounting for one's behavior can be deadly. Excuses like, "I didn't know how to call in sick" or "I was afraid to tell someone at work about my problems" are not good enough. Employers expect their people to let supervisors know if they can't make it to work. No-show, no-call remains the number one reason people are fired. Never leave important matters to someone else's imagination. Silence won't do when it comes to your job. Always speak up and say something:

- Call if you can't be there.
- Ask if you don't know.
- Ask for assistance if you need it.
- Speak out if you have a problem.
- Speak up if you have an idea.

Keeping quiet is rarely the answer in other situations either. Staying mute and motionless might get attention at a protest. A silent sit-in may make a point, but it takes talk—or verbal and non-verbal communication—to make real changes.

3. Emotional Communication

Feelings aren't facts, psychologists will inform you, but the fact that other people have feelings should never be overlooked in interpersonal communications. Emotions on fire usually burn someone. Any individual who is emotionally out of control can easily cause a conflagration. If you're unable to contain your emotions, you should take a deep breath, relax and wait for a better time to deliver your message. Writing it out, rather than spilling it out, relays words more rationally, too, when emotions run high.

Your words, facial expressions, gestures and voice all evoke feelings or emotions in others. If you enter a conversation in a moment of sentiment or passion, you're likely to say or do the wrong things. While you may be able to use appropriate words, your body language will betray you. It's better to wait until you've calmed down to engage in any discourse. Individuals with poor people skills plunge right in, no matter what their frame of mind or state of emotion. Imagine how this reporter feels while interviewing starlets who often indulge in unbridled emotion:

Examples:

Reporter: "What's the most important thing your fans should know about you?"

- "What kind of a stupid question is that?" snorts the first actor, glaring at her watch, then at the reporter.
- "You've got five seconds to find out what you want to know," growls the second actor under her breath, with one foot turned toward the door.

If either of these starlets were good people persons, they'd prepare a short, standard answer ready for reporters (*I'm a regular person, just like any of my fans.*) or ask to be excused until they're more rested and less rushed. Actors or public figures with enough human relations savvy will suggest another time and place to meet news writers for a statement.

When emotions are allowed to rule, good people skills collapse. Every apt people person learns to control his or her feelings when communicating with others, no matter how heated the situation. If his or her emotions are too unpredictable, it's in their best interest to delay encounters until they're ready to talk. People-ability means monitoring verbal, nonverbal and emotional elements of communication. If you always take other's feelings into account, as well as your own, you could become a first-class people person.

Example:

A fifth-grade teacher is angry that her students keep talking while they work. She lets her feelings about their behavior boil inside until she can no longer control her emotions. In a hot-tempered outburst, she screams: "Shut up! Now!"

By using disrespectful language and delivering her words with a high degree of emotion, an instructor may gain a few moments of quiet, but she loses her students' respect. Her control of the classroom diminishes with each outburst.

Verbal and non-verbal language, along with your emotional state, all work together whenever you communicate. If any of these elements are out of sync, you lose control of what you want to convey. Consider your reaction to the words, appearance or actions of these people:

1. **Which student is more likely to be praised to parents at conference time:**

   Student A: Yawns five or six times during each English class.

   Student B: Wears a bored expression, but is polite enough to pay attention.

   Student C: Leans forward in her desk to let her body language say: *Very interesting!*

2. **Which doctor would you chose to do your surgery?**

   Doctor A: Keeps back turned while describing your medical condition.

   Doctor B: Gives you absolutely no information about your upcoming surgery.

   Doctor C: Moves closer to look you in the eye while delivering good or bad news.

3. **Which attorney would you hire to represent you if you were wrongfully accused**?

   Attorney A: Chews gum while listening to details of your case.

   Attorney B: Walks toward the door like he's ready to leave while you're still talking.

   Attorney C: Leans across his desk and listens attentively while you explain your case.

4. **Which banker would you trust to invest your money?**

   Banker A: Keeps checking the computer screen while talking to you.

Banker B: Asks questions to clarify your meaning while you talk.

Banker C: Answers the phone and the door several times during your visit.

5. Which person do you trust to keep the company you work for from closing?

Corporate President A: Smiles and says hello to every employee at work.

Corporate President B: Is rarely seen or heard from by the majority of staff members.

Corporate President C: Wears a frown so threatening that employees duck to avoid him.

6. Which person would your dentist hire as a hygienist?

Dental Hygienist A: Chews gum while working on your teeth.

Dental Hygienist B: Wears her hair long and dangling from her shoulders.

Dental Hygienist C: Wears neatly cut, short hair and has a beautiful white smile.

7. Which person would you vote for as president?

Presidential Candidate A: Dresses like a fashion model.

Presidential Candidate B: Looks professional; usually appears in dark suit, white shirt.

Presidential Candidate C: Looks professional, but doesn't communicate ideas clearly.

8. Which person would you want to be your teacher?

Teacher A: Wears jeans and t-shirts to school just like her students.

Teacher B: Knows and uses all the latest slang to build trust with students.

Teacher C: Dresses, acts and speaks professionally in class and out of class.

9. Which sales person would you buy a car from?

Salesperson A: Wears gold chains to show off sales success.

Salesperson B: Sports a large tattoo of a martini on his/her forearm.

Salesperson C: Wears a shirt with a collar and nicely pressed pants.

10. Which person would you pay $100 an hour as a creative consultant?

Creative Consultant A: Slouches behind a desk full of clutter and unfinished work.

Creative Consultant B: Wears long, curly hair, but ties it back during the workday.

Creative Consultant C: Can't seem to maintain eye contact when talking to someone.

11. Which job candidate would you hire?

Candidate A: Dresses professionally but berates past employers at every chance.

Candidate B: Goes into lengthy detail with every question you ask.

Candidate C: Dresses professionally and speaks in concise, professional language.

12. Which person makes the best parent?

Parent A: Raises his/her voice to show disapproval of the child's actions.

Parent B: Maintains eye contact until the child changes behavior.

Parents C: Slaps the child, since actions speak louder than words.

Rehearse. To be a better people person, understand the power of verbal, nonverbal and emotional communication. Plan ahead. Sound, act and look the part you want to portray.

1. Write a script. Jot down how you plan to look, what you plan to say, how you intend to say it and what body language you will use the next time you need to persuade someone.

2. Observe the appearance, words, tone of voice, emotions and body language of the next person who's able to sell you something.

Chapter 7

Sacred Cs of Communication

Zealous people persons strive to acquire significant Cs.

Not all good communicators practice good people skills, but all smart people persons cultivate good communication habits. They learn to use communication to their advantage in getting along with others. To examine the quality and/or effectiveness of your communications, measure yourself in each of the following areas, all beginning with the letter C:

1. Credibility. The likelihood that others will believe in you and what you have to say.

Are you credible? Are you believable? Do you appear to be trustworthy? Do friends and family follow your example? Do co-workers respect you? Does your community listen to you? Do you sound and look like you know what you're talking about?

Questions like these are in the back minds of everyone who meets you. In the first seven seconds of any encounter, others will notice how you're dressed, how well you're groomed and how your posture portrays you. Before leaving home, ask yourself: *Do I look right for the situation I'm in?* If not, you won't be taken seriously. You wouldn't put much faith in a psychiatrist wearing a t-shirt or a senator in a mini-skirt. It pays to give attention to what you wear to the office, to the classroom, to the pulpit, to the courtroom—or anywhere you appear in public.

Example:

A teacher wears jeans, tennis shoes and t-shirt to class. She slumps in, head down, staring at the floor. She instantly loses credibility with students. In seven seconds, they see someone who is unprofessional in the way she dresses. They notice that she slouches and stares at the floor, failing to show the confidence she needs to be respected for her expertise on the job.

Does how you look, including your attire, send the message you want other people to receive? What they see, as well as what they hear, will influence how other people perceive you. If you aspire to be a top-notch professional, yet show up in public too often wearing casual clothing and unkempt hair, your ambitions won't be enough to take you where you want to go. If you don't *appear* to be credible, you won't be. Your words won't count much if you don't look the part. When your clothing is dirty or wrinkled, too tight or too short, the wrong color or style for the occasion, too dressy, too gaudy or too casual, your message falls flat—no matter how meaningful your words. Do you wear the right thing for every occasion? Do you often overdress or wear only what feels comfortable? All these issues are important to your credibility. After you've passed the dress test, straighten your posture to make sure you're not slouching.

Other aspects of your appearance could sabotage your credibility. When you talk, do others listen? Do people seem to take you seriously? If your words often go unheeded—at school, in the office, or at home—take another look in a mirror. Is your hair styled attractively? Or is it straggly? Is your face clean shaven or full of shadows? Are your nails manicured or bitten down to the quick? Next examine your composure. Can you maintain your composure when you are under stress? Do you seem self-confident?

Your teenager won't take you seriously if you burst into his bedroom in your bathrobe to chew him out for missing his curfew last night. He'll find you even less credible if you're flailing your arms uncontrollably while ranting and raving or pacing back and forth. No matter where you are, the way you look reflects on what you say. You probably wouldn't vote for a representative who always wears sneakers with a suit, despite his frank confession that his arches had fallen. You'd expect him to solve the problem some other way. Likewise, you'd be leery of a lawyer who couldn't look you in the eye.

Appearance makes a notable impression and can never be under-rated, but there's more to being credible than how we look. It's natural to ask ourselves as we listen, "Is she being honest with me? Is he well-prepared? Are her words consistent with her actions? We measure the validity of each person we meet in many ways. We all want to know: *How seriously should I take this person?* Once you're sure that you look believable, turn your attention to your body language.

What kind of story do your body position, your movements, your facial expression and voice tone tell. Does your body communicate confidence? Are you standing or sitting erectly to illustrate that you believe in yourself ? Every movement you make, every stance you take means something to the people around you. If you're not sure of yourself, try using positive self-talk to gain poise and self-confidence before communicating your message. Tell yourself, "What I have to say is important." If you present yourself well, act with poise, look the part and show self-assurance, you're more than halfway to being credible.

> ### *Is the language you use as credible as you look?*

Your next logical concern: *Is your language as credible as you look?* Do your words portray a person who is qualified to comment on your subject? The use of slang, for example, erodes authority. A spokesperson for a reputable organization, say a hospital or university, should stick with standard English (or whatever language is preferred). Peppering your conversation with words like *Cool!* or *Wow!* creates havoc with your credibility in ordinary, everyday exchanges. Colloquial speech causes severe credibility loss in other places. Using slang at formal occasions erases your image as a professional spokesperson, expert or leader. You'd think twice before letting a dentist pull your teeth if he or she greets you with "Howdy" or gives you a high-five.

Do you use proper grammar when you speak? If you're not sure, you need to brush up on high school lessons. Complete sentences, good subject-verb agreement and proper pronunciation all count in both written and spoken communication. If a salesperson exclaims, "We *was* first in the market," you'd find it hard to believe. Good grammar is associated with success. Saying "I *ain't* kidding" convinces no one that you're telling the truth. It doesn't sound credible.

Do you lapse into foul language, clichés or catchwords when you talk? Do you insert, *like,* or, *umm,* in sentences or interrupt your own thoughts with meaningless sounds or empty noises? Do you rely on over-used expressions, such as *You see, You know,* or *And, then* to tie your story together? Do you punctuate strong feelings with swear words, starting every other sentence with *Hell, or Damn,* for example? All these bad habits become credibility killers.

Saying too much can be just as dangerous as using expletives. If you feel you owe someone advice on their hairstyle, home decorating or choice of friends, think twice before you tell that person what to do. Just because you don't care for bleached-blond hair, carpeted floors or karma doesn't mean everyone else needs to follow your cue. You'll be more credible if you allow others their own preferences and avoid sounding like a know-it-all.

On the other hand, if a friend or acquaintance engages in behavior that could be harmful, like drinking and driving or smoking three packs a day, it's all right to say something—but say it with tact. Speak your mind cautiously. Shouting, "Are you crazy to consider driving in your condition?" or demanding, "You've got to give up cigarettes!" illustrate the wrong approach. Your good intentions will only bring on backlash unless you give advice in a way that keeps you credible in the eyes of others. "I'm concerned about your health" or "I'm afraid for your safety" make better conversation starters.

Rate Yourself: Rate the credibility or believability you have with other people. Assign the number that best describes your progress in each example.

1   2   3   4   5

Never   Sometimes   Always

1. ____ I dress appropriately for the situation I'm in.
2. ____ I use positive self-talk to give myself the confidence I need to be respected.
3. ____ I avoid slang, swear words, clichés and catchwords when I speak.
4. ____ I'm aware of what my body is doing whenever I speak to someone.
5. ____ I avoid wearing emotions on my face, no matter how bad my personal problems.

My score ____ If your score is lower than 25, keep trying to improve your credibility.

2. Content. The body or main message you want to communicate.

Is your message important enough to deliver? Or do you blah, blah, blah about anything and everything? Does your content match the situation you're in? Are your words relevant? Is the core of your message true? Is it accurate? Will your content be interesting or noteworthy to your listeners? Aside from idle chit-chat, anything you talk about should be worth saying.

The content of your message needs to be on target and aligned with the purpose of your communications. Do your words have a purpose? Are your words informative? Interesting? Necessary? If not, that's your cue to keep quiet. Otherwise, you risk the seedy reputation of *talking just to hear yourself talk.* If you keep chattering whether you have something relevant to say or not, other people will label you as an egotist, a narcissist or a foolish individual. If you're tempted to fill every pause, space or silent moment with empty talk, don't do it. There's nothing worse than listening to a compulsive communicator go on and on about nothing.

Worse yet is the guy who constantly complains. Even the closest of friends hate to hear complaints passed off as conversation. Grievances make poor content for communication. Keep your life's disappointments or your plain old bad luck to yourself. Avoid grumbling about everything from the weather to your representatives in Washington. Outlining all your aches and pains or repeating each of your recent exploits can be just as boring to the person sitting next to you. Instead, wrap your words around your listeners' interests, activities and goals. A good way to get to that point is to start any discussion with questions, not comments.

"How is your day going?" usually works pretty well. When it's your turn to talk, be brief but be sure to include all pertinent details. Your content should include all the facts. Your thoughts should be complete to ensure understanding, yet concise to prevent dominating the discussion. Five Ws and H of journalism set the standard for reporting news. They work as well for planning the content of any communication. Most comprehensive messages cover Who, What, When, Where, Why and How.

Examples:

Our family plans to fly to Florida in January to visit Disneyworld.

Your auto dealer advises you to come in to change your oil soon.

Your statement doesn't have to be long to include all relevant information. If you skip entire words or thoughts and pass on only sketchy information, though, your content is incomplete.

A coffee-house comment like "They don't know what they're doing in Washington" does not provide enough information. First of all, *who* doesn't know what he's doing? Second, *What* is it that the person or group doesn't know? And finally, *where* in Washington do you mean? Is it the President who doesn't know enough about the economy to keep Washington out of debt? Or do you mean Sen. Joe Statesman who doesn't know enough about the economy to keep all of us out of debt? Don't skimp on supporting details. Say exactly what you mean. Otherwise, your point may be lost in translation.

To make clear conversation, avoid relying too heavily on pronouns (he, they, we) or clichés (Washington vs. our government, our President, our Senator). Don't assume that every listener understands concepts that are commonly used but have more than one meaning. For example, consider the word *Washington.* Does it mean the state, the city, the first president? Or do you really mean the current government, the current President or the Congress?

Rate Yourself. Rate your ability to communicate meaningful content as you speak. Assign the number that best describes your progress in each example:

1   3   5

Never   Sometimes   Always

1. ___ Do you limit most of your message to things that matter?
2. ___ Is the content of your conversation informative or interesting?
3. ___ When talking to others, do you avoid airing all your gripes?
4. ___ Do you include all the relevant facts when passing on news to others?
5. ___ Do you only use pronouns (he, she, they, it) after you've first introduced the noun?

My score ___. If your score is lower than 25, keep trying to improve your content.

3. Candor. Speak honestly from your heart, without pretention or prevarication.

Are you candid? Are you sincere? Do you *tell it like it is?* Rules of candor include openness, honesty and truthfulness, along with good intentions. Sincerity means that what you say comes from your heart. You talk about what you believe in, rather than what you think people want to hear. Forthrightness and straightforwardness also lead to communicating with candor.

If you can't tackle unpleasant topics or feel you need to gloss over unsavory details, you are not candid. If you tend to downplay certain issues or downright lie about other things, you should question your own candor. Being candid means that you're open and frank with people. You're not afraid to deliver bad news or take on squeamish topics. When you use candor, you tell a truth that needs to be told. When you aggressively blurt out someone else's imperfections, however, you lack good judgment. Going too far in telling the truth is more often construed as blunt or outspoken, not candid. Acting nasty has nothing to do with candor.

Be candid, not critical, cruel or careless

Be candid, not critical, cruel or careless. Some occupations and professions require complete candor. Doctors can't sugar coat the truth about a patient's health. Expert witnesses could be prosecuted for breaking the law if they lie on the stand. Both need to be honest, but there's a kind way to be candid and a cruel way. If you choose the wrong route, you could do more harm than good.

Example:

A college professor realizes that an eager organic chemistry student lacks intellectual capacity to continue in a pre-medicine curriculum. The student failed both mid-term and final exam and can never give an accurate answer to a question in class.

If his professor communicates with candor, he will pull the student aside and tell him that his test scores don't bode well for a career in medicine. The professor will candidly advise the student to consider a different career path in an area where he does much better academically. If he is kind and considerate, without berating the student or belittling his performance, he is candid.

If you always consider the other person's feelings, you can be truthful, as well as tactful. You will be able to deliver difficult news while remaining a good people person. Start by showing empathy. Continue by telling your friend, family member or co-worker the bad news. To show support or sympathy, take steps like these to help soften the blow:

1. Provide a framework for details. *You've probably heard that sales are down.*
2. Use plain language and uncomplicated sentences. *We have to lay off staff.*
3. Speak softly and slowly, keeping eye contact. *That will be . . . unfortunate.*
4. Provide a nugget of hope. *I'll be glad to write you a good recommendation.*

When candor is called for in any situation, good people skills are critical. If the pre-med professor (above) skirts around the student's poor performance by giving insincere feedback, his lack of candor could be harmful. If he had put forth only the usual platitudes, such as, "You'll do better next time," or "Give it another try next semester," he would have deceived the student and done a great disservice. Repeating a course is costly and time-consuming—and unlikely to turn a failing student into the A or B candidate required to pass the next-level course.

Another candor question to ask yourself: Do your words have integrity? Do you ever say things just to sound good, even though they don't reflect your true feelings? People running for office often try to fake their real feelings. Their personal belief systems, however, aren't in line with what they portray, so they will surely slip in public sometime. If a politician proclaims an anti-poverty platform, but lives a lavish lifestyle, his paradoxical behavior will eventually surface somewhere. His high-priced clothing, high-rent housing, luxury vehicles and other expensive tastes will sooner or later be discovered by voters. More examples of comments that lack integrity include:

- Supervisors who swear the company has to cut back, then host elaborate parties
- Religious zealots who moralize to others while keeping dark personal secrets
- Parents who tell their teens not to use drugs, but do it themselves

Lack of candor can taint a whole picture or sneak through cracks in small pieces. It's best to stay away from exaggeration, gossip and slander. Whether accurate or inaccurate, lapses like these cause decreases in credibility.

Keeping all your facts straight is especially important in job interviews. If everything you claim doesn't corroborate with your résumé, you're sunk. If dates on your application differ from those on your vita, or achievements you describe in an interview are contradicted by a past employer, you're out of luck. Any small item that deviates from the truth can stop you from taking the next step on your career ladder.

> **Example:**
> An over-eager job candidate claims to have earned a half-million dollars in sales commissions at his previous company. When interviewers do the math, his claim turns out to be an exaggeration, not possible to reach at the candidate's former commission rate and the cost of products he sold. Puffed-up earnings figures may sound good, but often make the job candidate look like a liar.

Job candidates are far better off sticking to the plain truth. However, they should be careful about how far they go in telling the truth. Any kind of gossip, even if true, should never be passed on in your communications. Look at the example, again, of interviews. Candidates are often asked questions to measure how candid they can be without slandering someone else. A typical interview item to test this combination: *Tell us about someone who was hard to get along with at your past place of employment.*

Without knowing how far to go with candor, you could kill your chances of being hired by incorporating office gossip into your response. Never mention names or titles. Put the focus on the project, not the person. Responses that include elements of office gossip always make you look more like a fool than the person you're defaming.

Example:

"There was an old busybody in my office who kept track of everyone's whereabouts. No one liked her. She took notes whenever you left your desk and probably reported the time away from our desks to a supervisor. No one knows for sure why she was always spying on everyone, but we all hated it. No one, including myself, wanted to work with her."

Make sure you resist incriminating anyone you've worked with in the past. It's only hearsay, an attorney would plead. Stick with the facts, a news writer would add. Be selective in the stories you repeat, a career coach would insist. You're better off telling a more tasteful tale of a co-worker who always missed deadlines or who couldn't be counted on to complete his part of a project. To show that your claims are true, give examples of projects that went awry because someone else didn't hold up his end of the bargain. No matter how exasperating your fellow workers may have been, never dwell on the details. It will always sound like gossip. Talking endlessly about you and your experiences can be just as deadly as saying too much about others. Being candid doesn't mean cleansing your soul.

Rate yourself. Rate your ability to be candid or honest in what you say to everyone. Assign the number to each statement that best describes your progress.

1   3   5

Never   Sometimes   Always

1. ___ Is everything you say absolutely true?
2. ___ Do you pass on gossip or risk slandering someone?
3. ___ Are you guilty of exaggeration?
4. ___ Are your compliments and comments always sincere?
5. ___ Are you open and honest, even about things you don't like to talk about?

My score ___. If your score is lower than 25, keep trying to improve your candor.

4. Clarity. Choose and use words that your listeners will understand.

Does your message have clarity? Can it be clearly understood by everyone in your audience? Can all of your listeners relate to what you're talking about? Have you adjusted your communication to the crowd? Before speaking your first word, consider how well the people who hear you will comprehend the vocabulary you use. Ask yourself questions like:

1. What is the median education level of my audience?
2. What do my listeners usually read or watch on TV?
3. Who do they communicate with during the course of the day?
4. Which vocabulary words are likely to be used by my audience?
5. Are my words geared to the gut level of my listeners?

Use the KISS concept. KISS stands for "Keep It Super Simple." Keep your sentences short in casual conversation or in speeches, presentations and other public appearances. Keep your vocabulary easy to understand. Using every four- and five-syllable word you know hinders, rather than helps, sending messages to any kind of audience. Ordinary words will do. Don't put on airs or be pretentious for anyone. Even people with PhDs appreciate brevity and clarity.

Beware of acronyms. Never use abbreviations outside your tight little circle of peers who positively know the words behind letters like MEAP, UTI, IRS, SRI, AP, UPI or URL. Double check: Do my words include professional jargon that means nothing to the average person? Using mysterious acronyms can be especially offensive in interpersonal communication. If your doctor tells you, "Your BP is fine, but our LND-test discovered a 322-UTI that could cause ABC-XYZ," you'd probably be tempted to find a new physician. Professionals should always ask themselves: Will my patients or clients know what I mean? Is my listener capable of understanding my message? Does my audience need prior knowledge of my subject to understand it? If an accountant declares at a Chamber of Commerce meeting that the new tax code is unfair, she should predetermine: *Do all members know what's in the new tax code?* Probably not. In that case, her presentation should start with an explanation.

Actual formation of words in your mouth covers another aspect of clarity. Every communicator needs to enunciate, or pronounce words as distinctly as possible. If you find yourself often asked to repeat what you said, you may need to take more care in how you structure your words as they exit your mouth. Try opening your jaws a little wider. Form each letter of the alphabet carefully. Don't let sounds slur together or words escape in a flat manner because you're not using all your mouth muscles. Open wide and practice the familiar Broadway phrase: *How now brown cow.* Try other tongue twisters, such as *She sells sea shells by the sea shore.* Don't let the clarity of your communication become distorted through lazy lips.

Rate yourself. Rate your ability to communicate clearly. Assign the number to each statement that best describes your progress:

1   3   5

Never   Sometimes   Always

1. ＿＿ Do you open your mouth and form sounds carefully when talking?

2. ___ Do you practice the KISS theory with everyone you speak to?

3. ___ Do you avoid using acronyms your listeners might not know?

4. ___ Do you provide prior knowledge needed to understand every concept?

5. ___ Do you always say what you mean—and mean what you say?

My score ___. If your score is lower than 25, keep trying to improve your clarity.

5. Conciseness. Keep communication concise and crisp.

Do you get to the point quickly? Do your thoughts flow in a meaningful direction or do you meander? Can you deliver a message without digressing? There's nothing worse than listening to someone who goes on and on about everything but the topic at hand. Does every statement you make connect to your content, or relate to your story? Can you stay with a subject or do irrelevant ideas seem to slip off your tongue, ramble on and run off the track? The ability to be concise will make you a better people person. You'll take up less of everyone's time, focus on what's most important and make more sense when you have something to say.

Most adults can only listen attentively for 28 seconds or less before their minds start to wander. If you can't make a valid point in 28 seconds, all extraneous words should be scratched. Remove excess baggage. You should be able to cover two or three complete statements in that time. In conversation, your third remark is your cue to give the floor to someone else. Before delivering other kinds of messages, it pays to plan. Outline a full hour speech with vital facts, not extra or unnecessary fillers. Super Bowl Sunday ads, the best on TV, usually contain the fewest words. Any message has more impact on others when you know how to cut it to make it succinct.

> *The typical teenager tunes out after seven seconds.*

The typical teenager tunes out much sooner than the 28 seconds allowed for adults. You have just about seven seconds, so use your timeline with teens wisely. Make your message as short as possible. Forget the fluff. If a parent provides a teenager with a lengthy dissertation on responsibility before getting to the point of driving safely, the message is likely to be missed. In a fraction of a minute, mom or dad can squeeze in two or three short, life-saving, suggestions. Why waste words of warning by taking too long to present them? What a parent really needs to say to a son or daughter about driving is simple:

- Observe speed limits and other traffic laws.
- Pay attention and keep your eye on the road.
- Be responsible and drive carefully.

The younger your audience, the briefer your messages should be. On the other end of the spectrum, keep communications curt and clear with the elderly as well. A 90-year-old will fall asleep if your story takes too long.

Rate yourself. Rate your ability to be concise. Assign the number to each statement that best describes your progress:

1   3   5

Never   Sometimes   Always

1. ___ Do you get to your main point in a minute or less?
2. ___ Do you weed out excess words?
3. ___ Do you limit words to only what's necessary to say?
4. ___ Do you avoid rambling on about nothing?
5. ___ Do you apply the KISS theory to casual talk and formal speeches?

My score ___. If your score is lower than 25, keep trying to make your messages more concise.

Chapter 8

21ˢᵗ Century Communication: Less Can Be More

Adjust the scope of your comments for today's complicated world.

Radios boom while we drive. TV sets blare away all day in our homes. Background music breaks our concentration in offices, restaurants and other public places. Computers click. Phones ring. Canvassers call. There's chatter, chatter everywhere, so how does anyone get a word in edgewise? Communication comes at us from all sides. It's constant in the 21ˢᵗ century.

In a busy world, where at least 400 unsolicited messages a day reportedly reach out to us, everyone needs to let up a little. Limiting sentences to short clips may be the best way to communicate in a complicated world where overstimulation seems to be the norm. TV personalities, politicians and pundits know how to do it. They squeeze their messages into sound bites, or small bits of information, that listeners can catch on the run (or on the ride). Less can be more in most 21ˢᵗ-century communication.

Today, many of us are just too busy for idle talk in any setting. The days of passing time with friends on the front porch are long gone for most of us. There's little leeway and less patience for listening to flowery orations or long monologues. Everyone seems to be preoccupied with earning a living, doing household chores, raising kids, staying in shape, contributing to the community and trying to enjoy a few leisure activities. Commutes last longer and family members are further away. Great oratory skills meant more in Julius Caesar's time or even Abraham Lincoln's—when folks lived in villages with fewer distractions, little entertainment and no electronic devices. In the 21st century where there's always so much to do, story spinners often annoy others.

One way to cope with current conditions is by learning how to speak in *key messages*. This strategy helps you express your thoughts succinctly by reducing your initial comments to basic information. Newspaper reporters have been doing it for years. The opening line in every news article pretty much sums up the story. The lead sentence sticks to the facts: *Who, What, When, Where, Why* and *How*. Journalists add related details later in descending order of importance. Subscribers are free to quit reading after a few lines or to continue. It's up to them—and how much time they have at the moment.

Good people persons adopt a style on similar models. When they have something to say, they put all necessary words into small, but comprehensive, chunks. They dole out information in appropriate quantities for today's fast-paced world. Many good communicators rely on key messages to minimize words and maximize meaning. Key messages cover important ideas in a single sentence, followed by details on demand.

After making their first statement, these people allow listeners to add input, ask questions or make comments. They fill in the blanks in manageable bits. This kind of communication requires planning ahead.

Using key messages can be the best way to communicate among friends over coffee, while solving problems at work and in many other situations where people get together to accomplish a goal. Some savvy people persons always write out key messages and talking points in advance. Then, they know just what to say at the right time. Outlining important message(s) for meetings with colleagues or work groups ensures that all essential points are made and keeps everyone on task. After taking a few minutes to plan their first few key messages, most communicators find that this method becomes second nature in most verbal exchanges with people or groups.

Sample Key Messages:

Key Message #1:	National tests are not the best way to measure what students know.
Talking Points:	*(Added in response to questions, comments or other input)*
	• Standardized tests are expensive.
	• Giving these tests is time-consuming for teachers and students.

- The validity of such tests is currently under question.
- Educators have lost confidence in one-size-fits-all.
- Delays and errors in test results hold up informed decision making.
- Delays and errors in test results hold up college scholarships.

Key Message #2: Our family needs to eat dinner together every night.

Talking Points:
- It's too hard to plan meals when everyone's schedule is different.
- Trying to keep food warm and tasty for hours is almost impossible.
- We need to set a time for dinner that is convenient for everyone.
- I suggest we move it to 7 pm, since everyone is home by then.

Whether you have an idea to improve family life or you're trying to change the education system, using key messages makes sense. It's easy to pick random topics that you feel strongly about and go on and on about them—but who has time to listen to your ruminations? Your way of thinking can be far more memorable and convincing if you know how to contain your suggestions to key comments.

Busy family, friends and co-workers respond better to information delivered in small morsels. You'll also fare better in interpersonal relations if you give others a chance to ask questions or offer input, rather than preaching to them. In the 21st century, it's not quantity, or how much you say, that matters. What counts is your ability to convey your ideas in a concise, convincing and considerate manner.

Rehearse: Write a key message on a topic you feel strongly about. Then add several "talking points" to provide details after your initial statement.

1. Your key message:

_____

Your talking points:

1. _____
2. _____
3. _____
4. _____
5. _____
6. _____

Chapter 9

The Lost Art of Listening

Good listeners want to hear what others have to say.

When you think of *communication,* you more than likely picture two or more people talking to each other. Or, perhaps, you see a speaker addressing an audience. Whether it's a person at a podium, a newscaster on TV or your next-door neighbor shouting to you across the driveways, communication takes place. Talking, or sending any kind of message, seems synonymous with communicating. Yet, most experts agree that there's an equally important ingredient in effective communication. That's receiving messages—or listening. Many believe that we should spend up to 70 percent of our time listening. Most of us don't.

> *Listening is a skill rarely developed to its full potential.*

Listening is a skill rarely developed to its full potential. While nearly everyone aspires to improve their speaking ability, most of us take our listening skills for granted. If you took a survey, 90 percent of respondents would probably tell you they'd like to enhance their ability to communicate. What they really mean is that they would like to express themselves better or turn themselves into better talkers. Very few, if any, would say they want to become better listeners.

It never occurs to some people that they often miss the message because they don't really listen to the messenger. Sounds swirl around in the air every time two or more people gather, but very few folks actually hear everything uttered. It's all too common for one person to be plotting a response rather than processing the words he hears. Instead of listening half the time or more, most people tend to talk, talk, talk. Listening appears to be a lost art. Common sense tells us that "the less we speak, the more we hear."

An effective way to listen is to use your EARS. Of course, you need the ones on the sides of your head, but try using these EARS along with those:

Explore: Look for main ideas, themes or concepts.

Analyze: Think about each important concept and what it means.

Review: Review main points—and request clarification if needed.

Summarize or paraphrase themes and main points to show you understand.

Pay closer attention to what other people say, and you will take a giant step in improving your people-ability. If you don't know what's on another person's mind, you can't relate to them, understand them or empathize with them. True people persons connect with others by listening carefully to them. When one individual takes over the talking role, others soon lose interest. The less talkative fellow drifts away from the discourse. His mind wanders. He starts looking for escape routes, often considering ways to end the encounter. To remain engaged in any conversation, all parties need to join in. While one person talks, the others listen. After a few observations, it's time to change roles. In the best examples of communication, each speaker passes on the *talking torch* to another member of the group after no more than two or three contributions.

Meaningful dialogue is a two-way street. Words should flow back and forth in both directions, just as traffic flows down a street or avenue. Conversationalists with good people skills grant each other at least equal speaking time. To practice elementary listening skills, a novice can start by intentionally leaving lulls in every conversation. Short breaks between sentences will give listeners space and time to ask questions, make comments, clarify meanings, add input. One-way talkers deny other people the chance to become part of the picture. Dialogue turns to monologue.

Two-way communications is vital to effective communication. Dialogue has grown so important in today's environment that traditional mass media, such as newspapers, radio and TV stations, have even caught on. Once just one-way channels of information, many media outlets have adopted two-way tactics with great success. Anyone who listens to their car radio hears constant examples. Fans now call in to report on everything from road conditions to their first dates or the worst thing their mothers made them wear to school. Many stations actually provide prizes for people who dial in to join the conversation.

Rehearse: The next time you tell a story or relay an experience to a friend, pause after each detail to give your friend an opportunity to ask a question or make a comment.

Chapter 10

Six Listening Styles for Six Situations

Listening techniques change according to occasion.

At a minimum, listening should be a 50-50 proposition. Some experts advise us to listen as much as 70 percent of the time, reserving just 30 percent of any discourse for ourselves. Fifty percent, 60 percent or 70? What's right when it comes to listening? Listening is situational. It depends on circumstances. We pay more attention to a lecture than we do to the music on our car radio, for example. We listen to our college professors differently than we would to a kindergarten class. Good listeners rely on six kinds of listening, appropriate for six different situations:

1. Casual Listening

Casual listeners keep working while conversing or may even remain in front of a computer while sharing thoughts with a co-worker in the next cubicle. Casual listening often takes place while groups of people multi-task or pay less than full attention to the topic at hand. When spouses, family members or co-workers mumble while meandering, their listeners are often preoccupied too. In casual listening situations, no one really expects anyone else's full attention. These exchanges include only jibber-jabber, or easy talk. Participants tune in sporadically through casual listening.

Example:

Mrs. X cooks dinner in the open atmosphere of her modern home. She makes an offhand remark to nobody in particular.

> "Everything should be ready in a few hours," she utters, no urgency in her voice.
> "Sounds good," responds Mr. X, without looking up from his newspaper.
> "Smells good," adds their adolescent who is outlining a history chapter at the dining room table.

Conversations like these take place in homes and offices around the world. It's the daily dialogue of people in close proximity to one another. Eye contact is not expected for casual listening. Active listening is not in order. As long as comments remain cursory, no one cares what's said or unsaid in these situations. A brief acknowledgement—or no response—is all that's required. Individuals involved in separate activities more or less talk to themselves, but others feel free to chime in if they'd like.

Problems arise in families or organizations when some members don't recognize casual listening. The one who tries to communicate more important information in such a setting ends up frustrated and angry because others aren't paying close enough attention. Those who continue to work, while casually quipping, resent more demanding interruptions that interfere with their concentration. If everyone recognizes the situation and no one attempts to make conversation more than casual, there's no problem. More serious comments can be saved for another time.

Review. In everyday situations, casual listening is quite common.

List two situations in everyday life where casual listening works:

1. _____ 2. _____

2. Social Listening

Social listening involves using the sense of hearing for enjoyment, relaxation or celebration. Social conversationalists make small talk, tell jokes, ask light questions, repeat news or simply banter words about to maintain relationships. They make gatherings more fun, groups more lively and special occasions more interesting. Social listening is more personal than casual repartee, but less than serious conversation. Short phrases like "Nice to see you" or "You're looking great" qualify as communication. At the same time, levels of listening lack the intensity of more meaningful discussions. Participants usually stand or sit face-to-face. Everyone feels comfortable tuning in, tuning out or taking turns talking. Social listening doesn't demand 100 percent involvement. It's not appreciated if used in workshops or theaters. Reserve social listening for cases that call for small talk or less-than-serious dialogue. Social listening is appropriate before and after meetings or performances, but not during them. It's perfect for parties, dinners, weddings, formal dances—even funerals. Most conversation at such events consists of short comments that break the ice, relieve stress or alleviate boredom. Light listening with an occasional nod or smile suffices.

Review: Social listening is most appropriate when people get together for fun or functions.

List two occasions in your life where social listening may be appropriate.

1. _____ 2. _____

3. Focused Listening

Use focused listening for situations where you really need to pay attention, to understand, appreciate or take home a message. Program interruptions on TV or radio provide the perfect example of the intensity of this kind of listening. You stop everything to hear important announcements at home, school or church. Similar attention is expected of anyone attending stage plays, symphonies, concerts or lectures. For people who go to the theatre to enjoy dramatic or musical performances, focused listening is fundamental. Catching all parts of the program is crucial to make the excursion worthwhile. Likewise, listening can be vital at meetings or conferences. It's the usual choice wherever people gather to gain information, to be trained or to accomplish something specific. Focused listening is intentional, strategic and narrowly channeled.

Think of focused listening as strategic listening. It's deliberate, calculated and premeditated. If you make an appointment with your doctor for diagnosis, your accountant to furrow through your finances or a salesperson to buy a new car, you plan to listen carefully. You intend to be discerning. Other events where you may need to give your undivided attention include meetings, conferences and seminars. Some fans prefer to use focused listening at football games, tennis matches and other sporting events as well. They don't want to miss any action. Typical occasions that call for focused or strategic listening include:

- Most events that require reservations or tickets
- Meetings or gatherings where there will be an agenda
- Any occasion that brings people together for a serious purpose

If something specific is on the agenda, an event probably provides enough motive for focused listening. Whenever two or more people get together to work on a project, discuss an issue or solve a problem, all participants should switch to focused listening. Unfortunately, many activities that require full attention, such as close sports games or top-notch performances, take place in noisy, irrelevant or less-than-desirable environments. These events still demand determined listening for attendees who want to reap desired results.

Example:

At concerts and other performances, most listeners prefer to put the center of their attention on the melody and words of songs or understand speakers or actors on stage. A lecture, an opera, a musical, a motion picture all require focused listening.

At important events, meetings or discussions, you'll want to hear details, evaluate what you hear and decide what to do with that information. If it's a musical you're watching, you need to hear all the lines and soak up all the songs to leave the theatre content. You want to get as much as you can for your money.

If you're taking part in a parent-teacher meeting, you'll want to know every detail of your child's progress. You need to listen carefully to decide if your son or daughter is learning at grade level. You need to understand clearly to be able to help your child with his lessons. You need to take everything in to go home satisfied about the school, the teacher and the curriculum. On occasions where strategic listening serves your purpose, you have to hear all the words before you can see the whole picture.

Review. Focused listening is required when hearing details is important.

Name two events or occasions where focused listening is required:

1. _____ 2. _____

4. Informed Listening

The point of informed listening, the kind carried on in most classrooms, is to:

- Learn a lesson
- Retain facts or details
- Understand important concepts

To accomplish goals like memorizing facts, understanding concepts or remembering details, listeners must:

- Pay attention to everything, including introductions
- Listen carefully to overviews, directions or recommendations from the instructor
- Mentally extract key words from clumps or clusters of information that is shared
- Ask questions to clarify details and correct misunderstandings
- Process information by making mental pictures or taking notes

Informed listeners know at the start of a class, lecture or lab session that they urgently need to retain much of the content that is provided. They'll use what they learn to solve problems, finish projects or show their proficiency on quizzes or tests. Consequently, informed listening skills could be elevated to a science.

Informed listeners need to zone in sharply on certain names, places and dates. Informed listeners have to remember main points and details. The best informed listeners clear their minds of distractions—irrelevant thoughts and ideas—before paying attention to the teachers, professors or workshop presenters delivering information. Some very good informed listeners go as far as to use meditation techniques to push random thoughts and concerns out of their heads before a session starts. Informed listening takes complete concentration.

To become well educated, well informed or ready to pass an exam, students need to open their whole minds to the person who is passing on knowledge. Their brains must be totally alert and attentive to the book, computer program, video or any other medium through which information flows. Outside of classrooms, though, informed listening can be just as significant. Informed listening is called for when work supervisors give instructions or hand out assignments, or when demonstrators explain how to operate a new piece of equipment.

Review. Learning lessons at school calls for informative listening.

A. What are some strategies for informative listening?
1. _____ 2. _____

B. Other than at school or at work, where is informed listening the best style to use?

1. _____ 2. _____

5. Purposeful Listening

Concentrating to make decisions, form opinions or alter beliefs can best be described as purposeful listening. Participants have a specific reason to hear a message. They need to use purposeful listening to understand fine points or critical information. Purposeful listeners have to hear beyond words. Their task is similar to *reading between the lines*. While engrossing themselves in a message, these listeners work diligently to interpret the meaning. Listening to a sermon is a prime example. Purpose-driven listeners look for special meanings in:

- Select words
- Repetition of words
- Meaningful stories or anecdotes
- The speaker's body language
- The speaker's tone of voice

When a preacher folds his hands in prayer or looks upward during a sermon, purposeful listeners mentally mark the moment as a time to listen closely and reverently. An inspirational pastor or speaker chooses words carefully, especially words with emotional connotations—those that evoke feelings in others, such as *peace, silence, serenity.* Parishioners, and other audiences react to words like *love, hope, charity* with their hearts as well as their heads. Emotional reactions help people internalize messages, or make them part of their own thoughts. Purposeful listeners prefer speakers who use anecdotes or stories.

Their goal is easier to grasp when the person in front of them makes a story more dramatic, adds modulation or changes tone of voice for significant words. An audience of purposeful listeners can easily feel the message, along with hearing it. Speakers whose job is to evoke emotions master many techniques before taking the podium. These expert talkers make it easy for people to follow them. From opening awe-inspiring words, audiences follow a speaker's lead by shifting subconsciously to purpose-driven listening. The style of the speaker and the power of the message can make a big difference to purposeful listeners.

Another component of purpose-driven listening causes participants to evaluate messages they hear and assess them for honesty and accuracy, logic and value. Listening to politicians, for example, calls for such scrutiny, as consequences of their comments can be high. Really good purposeful listeners weigh words carefully before agreeing or reacting to something. When candidates repeat certain phrases, such as *prosperity for all*, many constituents respond positively. Good purposeful listeners, though, evaluate such platitudes carefully. They measure one set of words against others to determine which pithy remarks are plausible and which promises are possible. Purposeful listening can be extremely important during an election year. People who use it think twice before running out to vote for everyone who uses powerful or provocative language.

Selective hearing should be used as well in other high-stakes cases. Advertising pitches, proselytizing messages and other attempts to influence us require our discretion. Taking advice from sales people, doctors, lawyers and health or human services professionals should be done only after listening purposefully. It's the best way to hear to get help or make good decisions.

Often a speaker's theme, main ideas, inflections and key words are all carefully calculated to convince others. Phrases like "Act now!," or "Last chance to make a difference," or "Your best choice is . . ." evoke action from people who may fear being left out, left behind or left for dead. Good purposeful listeners understand the power of words on emotions and never let fancy phrases fool them. On the other hand, purpose-driven listening can work as an inspiration or motivator in the right situations.

Review. Purposeful listening is best when interpretation is needed or inspiration is wanted.

Describe a time when you relied on purpose-driven listening:

_____

_____

6. Sympathetic or Responsive Listening

Sympathetic listening takes place between close friends, family members or people who are comfortable enough with each other to share their deepest thoughts and emotions. Relationships suffer when this kind of interpersonal interaction occurs only rarely or never. All human beings experience moments of anguish when soothing words from a close companion can mean more than anything else. Sympathetic listening is also practiced by counselors, psychiatrists and psychologists. Such professionals train to listen well and respond appropriately to their clients or patients.

The idea behind sympathetic listening is usually to help someone with problems to be solved or issues to be examined. This type of therapeutic listening is familiar to anyone who has ever visited a counselor or mental health professional. In those situations, people pay specialists to listen properly. Practitioners allow their patrons to talk freely, while they listen actively (lean forward, nod the head, show empathy, use appropriate facial expressions). Most professional listeners leave 80 to 90 percent of the talking up to the individual he or she serves. This kind of listener needs to hear the other person's perspective without passing judgment, showing embarrassment or reacting negatively to what they hear.

Closely related to sympathetic listening is responsive listening, sometimes called active listening. Marriage and family counselors often recommend responsive listening for clients who find themselves in situations where communications have broken down. Counselors, clergy and psychologists advise their customers to start listening with full attention to rebuild fractured relationships. Married couples, parents and children top the list of people who strive to become better listeners by learning how to be more responsive to one another in close relationships. All parties need to learn how to show actively that they actually hear what was said, understood what was meant and take their spouse's or family member's message seriously. A few steps to successful responsive listening include:

1. Maintain EYE contact during the entire conversation.
2. LEAN forward or toward the speaker to show you are interested.
3. NOD occasionally to show that you understand or agree.
4. Ignore distractions that interrupt discourse.
5. Avoid changing subjects at all costs.

To show they care about the other person and truly want to understand their point of view, responsive listeners also should:

6. ASK questions to clarify meanings.
7. REPHRASE or REPEAT to ensure understanding.

Examples:

To maximize the results of responsive listening, employ the following elements of communication in every conversation.

- **Facial expressions:** Maintain a look of interest throughout the conversation.
- **Body language:** Use face muscles and hand gestures to indicate that you're getting the message.
- **Feedback:** Add occasional interjections to show that you are emotionally involved in the other person's issues (*aha, I see, really?*).

1. **Review.** Sympathetic or responsive listening is used to show empathy or compassion.

   When do people need this kind of listening? Give four examples:

   1. _____ 2. _____

   3. _____ 4. _____

Other important listening tips

Besides selecting the best listening style for every situation, good people persons pay attention to their surroundings whenever communication takes place. They check on everything from the temperature to lighting to room arrangement. To set the stage correctly, eliminate all distractions. Remove extraneous objects, such as piles of magazines. Reduce external static by choosing the quietest place for a particular conversation or presentation. Location, noise level, seating, spacing, etc., all come into play. Public relations people understand this principle better than anyone else. When they host a press conference or interview a speaker, they often spend hours just setting the stage.

Choose surroundings that maximize attention spans. Make sure that everyone will be comfortable in the place where you plan to deliver your message. Location seems to be as important in human relations as it is in real estate. It's never a good idea, for instance, to try to heal an injured relationship while walking through a busy mall or sitting in front of a blaring ball game on television. If you have something important to say at home, turn off the TV. Remove clutter from tables, couches and chairs in the room that will be used for conversation with company. Apply the old dinner-by-candlelight approach if that's what it takes to make communications with a loved-one more effective.

Internal distractions, such as exhaustion, hunger or preoccupation with problems also present barriers to meaningful communication. Avoid introducing serious subjects when you know the people you want to reach have homework to do, deadlines to meet or have regular activities scheduled. Plan your discussion at the right time of day when everyone's rested and fed. Good meeting leaders, workshop presenters and good hosts provide drinks or refreshments to prevent hunger attacks in the audience or parched throats from distracting participants. They also point out bathrooms and provide breaks to allow people to take care of personal needs.

Rehearse. Develop plans for a mythical meeting where everything possible is done ahead of time to minimize distractions and maximize listening potential for everyone attending the meeting.

Chapter 11

Sharpen Your People Skills

To handle problems, use your head. To handle people, use your heart.

By now you're probably on the right track: It pays to perfect your people skills. Persons with better-than-average interpersonal expertise are often considered the lucky ones by others who are less well-equipped. Good people persons are more likely to have friends and followers. They are often the ones to be hired first or promoted to higher positions at work. Of course, their competition will claim that gregarious go-getters buttered up a supervisor to get ahead. The truth is that it's hard to fake kindness and consideration toward others. However, it is possible to sharpen your interpersonal skills so people-ability seems to come naturally. Follow these five strategies and see how far they take you:

Strategy 1. Recognize the value of others

Start today. Seek out special gifts, or strengths, in everyone you meet. Find something noteworthy in each person who crosses your path. Make it a goal to look for silver linings in every purse or pocket. Be determined to discover something good in everyone, and you will. Keep in mind that it takes effort and attention to see the best in others. Practice being a specialty-seeker instead of a fault-finder. Look for the good in everyone until it becomes habit. Ask yourself at each encounter during the course of any day: *What does the butcher, the baker, the candlestick maker bring to the table?* To start recognizing the value in others, contemplate questions like:

- What can my neighbor do that I can't?
- Which person am I most likely to go to when I need help?
- Who's the most likely person I'd ask if I need something done in a hurry?
- Which person do I call when I need a pep talk?

Whether it's a mentor, an ally, a good friend—or even an enemy—each individual who comes into contact with you sews another square to the quilt of your life. Your brother-in-law may be a bragging buffoon, but if you stop to think about his best side for a moment, you might realize that he'd give the *shirt off his back* to you. He's the most generous fellow you know.

Many notable historical figures recognized the uniqueness of every human being. Abraham Lincoln, our best-remembered President, understood the individual worth of each person who landed on American soil. To Lincoln, slaves were not invisible, no more than property to be purchased by plantation owners, as many during his time believed. To him, people of all colors were human, each with special skills and abilities. It may have taken over 150 years, but eventually the majority in our country came to the same conclusion. As Lincoln once did, we realized that a black man blessed with exceptional speaking skill could be elected president.

Once you begin to see the intrinsic worth of everyone, it's easy to amble your way around the rough edges or over the cracks to notice the special gifts of ordinary people. Look for something good and you'll find it. Your cranky old neighbor may be a pain in the neck, be she grows the most beautiful roses in town. An odd looking man, wearing rags and begging for money, could be the kindest person you've ever met. Your paperboy may miss the porch occasionally, but if you look closely at his behavior you might see that he's the most polite young man on the block.

To progress as a people person, seek out unique qualities in the entire cast of characters in the drama of your life. Start showing appreciation for their contributions. Acknowledge the achievements of others. Thank repair persons for services rendered, pay sincere compliments for jobs well done, offer small donations to show support for anyone who is trying to help others.

Don't expect everyone you meet to be just like you. Search for signs that make each person distinctively him or her. Be on the lookout for special qualities. Even hardened criminals excel in some way. Some tap into their artistic talent or study the Bible or another holy book to become spiritual advisors to fellow inmates. Many prisoners turn around their lives behind bars by discovering their hidden talents. Keep in mind that all human beings blend together both blemishes and beauty. Developing your people skills by teaching yourself to see other's gifts gives you the grace to overlook no one.

Strategy 2. Preserve other people's self-esteem

"A big man is one who makes everyone else feel bigger when they're with him," someone wise once said. This clever statement provides a good guideline for preserving other people's self-esteem. A good people person makes everyone around him or her feel better about themselves, not worse. Treating others with respect rests at the peak of positive human relations. An individual with outstanding interpersonal skills is fair, decent and kind to everyone, despite their social status, economic circumstances or level of education. Put everyone else on a pedestal and they'll all look up to you.

There's never a good reason to embarrass, harass or make another person feel less valuable than you think you are. A people-person never points out peculiarities, or gets a laugh at someone else's expense. Even the *life-of-the-party* demonstrates poor people skills in making fun of others. Anyone who gets pleasure from putting people down eventually drives everyone away, especially bystanders who witness their bad behavior. Such predators may snare an occasional snicker from a crowd, but soon find themselves standing alone. No one wants to look foolish, feel inferior or watch another person squirm.

Put-down perpetrators repel others faster than a squirt of mosquito spray. Their cruel words, mocking body language and intimidating tone of voice can quickly crush someone else's confidence. While bullies may sometimes get away with bad behavior in schoolyards, their poor people skills are much more likely to be judged negatively in the adult world, especially in the workplace.

Handle problems with your head; handle people with your heart. You read a manual to restart a car with a dead battery. You use directions to assemble a bike. You rely on your common sense to keep cold air from coming in around the edges of your doors. It takes mechanical skill to fix a broken faucet and intellectual ability to analyze a problem.

Let your heart be your guide when dealing with people. A smile, a handshake, or a comment is often all it takes to ease pain, or put the spotlight on someone else. A few words of praise go a step further to affirm other people's importance. Insincere compliments don't count, but acknowledging another person's strengths builds their self-esteem.

> **Example:** A department supervisor may describe himself as "tough" for publicly humiliating employees who make mistakes, but he will be perceived by others, both above and below him, as unkind, uncaring and out to embarrass and demean the people around him.

A supervisor with good people skills must correct mistakes that are made by his subordinates, but it should be done in private, not in front of everyone else. Criticism should be constructive, rather than destructive.

Focusing on faults has the opposite effect. Even if criticism can't be avoided, pointing out another person's deficiencies should be done delicately. Make corrections with kindness.

Every good people person practices the art of preserving other people's self-esteem. It's often a matter of choosing positive rather than negative actions and words. Telling a child, "I'm happy when you want to be clean" sounds far better than saying, "You'll look like a pig if you don't take a bath." Some behaviors automatically affect people positively, while other actions guarantee a negative effect. A nod of the head or high-five with a hand says you approve. A grimace or frown, on the other hand, is usually interpreted as disapproval.

To recognize others is to accept them. All humans yearn to be accepted rather than rejected by others. When you make it a point to greet everyone, even children, at a family gathering, you not only preserve self-esteem but you also make other guests feel like part of the group. Each time you reach out a little further by stopping briefly to socialize with someone, you raise that person's sense of self-worth. Take an extra leap by asking everyone in the room, "How's your day going?" Each time you pause to listen to a few particulars of a person's life, you've taken a giant step toward building good people skills.

Strategy 3. Encourage others

Identify and praise the strengths of family members, co-workers, friends and neighbors. Encourage their dreams and show interest in their interests. Even if you're not an outdoors person and you can't stand getting your hands dirty, admit to the old man down the street that you admire his garden. Encourage him to enter his zucchini in the annual fair. Take home a few vegetables if he offers to give you some of his handiwork. Tell him later how much you enjoyed experimenting with a new salad or eating his spaghetti squash.

Congratulate your new supervisor—or any of your co-workers—on promotions. Compliment colleagues who meet project deadlines or develop great pieces of work. Praise your peers on their presentations, their programs or their progress—even though you may be a little bit envious. Don't over-do it or you'll look like a phony. Use compliments as needed.

Contrary to what you may think, you won't reduce your chances for success by supporting your competition. If you praise, encourage and prop up people around you, most will appreciate your generous spirit. They'll want to share their expertise with you. Your co-workers or family members are more likely to promote your interests, provide you with assistance and support your ideas in the future.

The hardest people to praise and encourage are often those closest to us. After many years of marriage, it's often difficult to see the day-to-day efforts of our spouses or our children. We appreciate our parents only after years away from them. You may have to set goals to practice preserving self-esteem in your household. Several ideas include:

- Compliment a family member's good fashion sense. Be sure to notice when your spouse spruces up for a special event or a son or daughter dresses especially well.
- Mention how much you appreciate the mundane—taking out the garbage, loading the dishwasher, shoveling the driveway—or a million other small steps someone takes to make your life more comfortable.
- Take family member's interests seriously. You may not enjoy playing golf or going on Saturday shopping excursions, but give your loved ones the space to pursue what pleases them. Encourage them to explore and expand their horizons.
- Share excitement for others' successes. Celebrate your son's A in math or your daughter's lead role in the school play.

Strategy 4. Show empathy for others

Pay attention to what's going on in the lives of people who surround you. If friends, neighbors or family members have lost their jobs, their homes or their spouses, for example, don't be afraid to let them know that you sympathize with their loss. Put yourself in their shoes. Try to feel their pain. Too often, we remove ourselves from anyone experiencing bad luck. We act like their problems could be contagious, instead of showing them that we understand their predicament and would like to help.

Real people-persons try to be available to others when they can. Even in every day circumstances, try to be more aware of other people's needs and wants. If it looks like a co-worker is overwhelmed with end-of-year reports and needs a hand, ask what you can do to lighten the load. Their assignments may not be in your job description, but there's got to be something you can do to give them a hand. Picking up lunch while letting them work could be the answer. The problem may not even be in your department, but occasionally taking a few minutes for someone else makes you a better people person.

In the study of psychology, Abraham Maslow's hierarchy provides a few tips on what all people need. The bottom step on his ladder covers physiological needs, such as body comfort, food, water, sleep, etc. Keeping those around you comfortable meets at least one need. On the next wrung, Maslow places physical safety. When folks feel threatened by harm they function less fully, according to Maslow. Then he adds love, affection, sense of belonging and self esteem to the next levels. Only when all those needs are met on subsequent steps, he believed, can people realize their full potential. Maslow's Hierarchy of Needs can be controversial, but most psychologists agree that we all do better once we've satisfied our basic needs. Good people persons become aware of what others around them need to flourish.

Take a moment to consider other people's *wants*, as well as their *needs*. If a spouse or family member talks constantly about a dream house, for example, it's not a good idea for someone else to take away that dream with statements like, "Don't even think of it. We can't afford it." When your business partner tells you he'd like to run for President some day, don't laugh. Instead, acknowledge your partners' wants: "I know how badly you'd like to build that house" or "I admire your ambition to run for office."

Rather than ruling out someone's dream, ask that person what it would take to be able to afford that house, that boat or that BMW. Beseech your business partner to tell you more about his political aspirations. He may never run for president of anything, but he'll feel better about himself if you take his dreams seriously. Children are especially vulnerable to ruined fantasies and dashed dreams.

Some things our loved ones want are impossible to achieve, but their desires should not be denied. Admit that you understand how they feel about their dream. "I know you want it. I wish we could afford it" is much better than "Forget it—we can't afford it." Like Native Americans, walk in the other person's shoes. How would you feel if someone close to you made fun of your plans for the future? This advice is especially important for family members. Chasms grow between teens and their parents, for instance, when adults can't put themselves in the young person's place. A broken-hearted 16-year-old won't feel better when a careless parent makes comments like:

- "Just get over it."
- "I hope you're not going to mope around forever."
- "Snap out of it."
- "You're too young to take someone so seriously, anyway."

A wise mother or father acknowledges that their child feels sad about a breakup—even though the parent may have realized that the match was disastrous. It's always better to accept their feelings and respond with statements like:

- "It's always tough to end a relationship with someone you like."
- "I can see this breakup is hard on you."
- "I'm sorry for your loss."

A good question to ask when you're around someone who seems unhappy, uneasy or under a lot of pressure: "What can I do to brighten your day?" Knowing that you notice how they look is sometimes enough to restore self-esteem when people appear sad or discouraged. Many negative feelings stem from fear of inadequacy.

Strategy 5. Build trust

Assured reliability based on the character, ability, strength or truth of someone or something. That's a standard dictionary definition of trust. Trust or confidence makes living together and working together possible. When people doubt their own ability or don't believe they can count on others around them, anger and anxiety often surface. Without trust, paranoia sets in. You start to think:

- Your boss is out to get you.
- A relative is buttering you up to borrow money.
- Your children only visit to take advantage of you.
- Your husband or your wife wants to control you.
- Your colleagues are trying to sabotage your work.

Trusting other people can be risky. (*If we trust someone, we could get hurt*). Putting faith in another human being can lead to pain. (*What if I love him and he leaves me?*) or cause anxiety (*I'm afraid I'll never have enough money to marry her*). Lack of belief in oneself usually expresses itself in anger—self anger. Not trusting someone else also leads to anger, along with misunderstanding, low morale and people-ability mistakes.

To create trust where there is none (or not much), start with low-risk behaviors, such as making small talk or paying a sincere compliment. You also inspire trust by listening attentively to others. Drifting off in another direction while listening to someone is sure to interfere with their faith in you. To build trust in all your relationships, learn and observe the following do's and don'ts. Apply them in your home, your office, at school and in community or work groups:

DO . . . .
- Maintain eye contact. Looking away tells others they're not important.
- Call people by their names. The sweetest word in any language: someone's name.
- Ask for others' opinions. Next in importance to a person's name is his opinion
- Say thank you. Show you're grateful for everything other people do for you.
- Introduce people. Always make sure all people in a group know each other.
- Welcome everyone. Acknowledge everyone's presence, even if you're not host.

DON'T . . . .
- Criticize—instead, suggest better ways to do things.
- Ridicule by making a public example of someone's errors.
- Condemn an individual or a group by labeling them (lazy, freeloaders, etc.).

- Try to change people. Build from their strengths and downplay their weaknesses.
- Make excuses. "I've been really busy" (too busy for them, in other words).
- Hold grudges against anyone.
- Break trust by going against your word.

Trust is impossible to build without trustworthiness. If you are shifty, shaky or sure to disappoint people in your path, you'll find it difficult to convince others to have confidence in you. An act as small as forgetting to make a promised telephone call destroys trust. People who don't show up for appointments or miss meetings or parties after they've RSVP'd quickly break down belief in their integrity.

To make yourself trustworthy, say what you mean and mean what you say. Trust works hand-in-hand with good communication. Without it, there is no real communication or camaraderie. If you say "I love you" every day to your partner, but he or she can't trust you to be faithful to them, your words mean nothing.

If you're sure you can't trust anyone but yourself, you'll never be able to rely on others. If you hold grudges or hold in anger for days at a time, rather than starting each day as a new one, you're likely to inhibit your ability to be at ease in any environment. If there's only play-acting between people in your office or in your home, there's no real trust. You're all in trouble, because confidence in others is the bond that builds understanding, ownership and cooperation.

Trust is "the glue of life," claimed Steven Covey, author of *Seven Habits of Highly Effective People.* Without this adhesive, communications falter and relationships become fragmented. Trust builds relationships and holds people together. Marriages end when one partner can't trust the other to be faithful or to be frugal with family funds. A work team without trust can't depend on one another, expect all players to do their part or take pride in their joint progress. As a result, products turn out sloppy, customer satisfaction drops, business declines and companies fail.

Remember

- Trust builds relationships and holds them together.
- Without trust, there is no real communication or camaraderie.
- Trust is impossible to build without trustworthiness.
- Put your trust in others if you want their confidence in you.

Recall. Recall a situation where you lost trust in a person, product or company. What would it take to rekindle your faith in them? Be specific:

Chapter 12

Build Bonds from the Beginning

You never get a second chance to make a first impression.

Whether you're introducing yourself to a stranger, making an initial contact with a customer or new employee, meeting your in-laws for the first time or joining a new group, trust starts developing (or declining) from the beginning. Your first 10 seconds together determine how difficult it will be to build bonds—or if there will ever be bridges between you. Be aware of your impact on others from the get-go. Their faith in you as a person is something you need to earn. You can't buy it, fake it or force it.

You inherently know this to be true when you plan and prepare for first encounters with anyone. Think about the effort you put into getting ready for your first date. Girls usually spend hours plotting scenarios with a best friend. Some actually rehearse what they are going to do and say. Most mentally go through their closets. Females are also likely to try on dozens of different outfits for just the right look. Males may do a little research online or in magazines or ask an older man for advice. Young people know they need to look and act their best to make a good impression. Even couples who meet and marry in their 80s, understand the process.

What you do, what you say and how you appear in the first few seconds set the stage for future relationships. Your new cohort will size you up, just as you form an instant impression of him or her. His broad smile makes you feel instantly comfortable, or his stiff manner may activate your anxiety. Her beauty may dazzle you or her inch-thick make-up might scare you. Any early image is likely to remain in the mind for a long time.

You never have a second chance to make a first impression. Attire, body posture, gestures and facial expressions all work together to create a composite. Initial words or comments enter the picture, too. Most people know that grooming, deportment and dress count, but many don't know what to say when initially introduced to someone There are several simple steps to starting conversation. Use them to help you make the best possible first impression. Here's a five-step formula to follow in any early encounter.

1. Start talking about low-risk topics such as the weather or non-controversial news.

    "Are you looking forward to spring?"
    "What's your favorite season?"
    "What do you know about the new building going up on the corner?"

2. Listen actively to the other person's responses.

Show interest through your face and gestures.
Nod. Smile. Engage. Laugh. Enjoy.
Maintain eye contact with the other person.

3. Ask questions that draw the other person in:

"Did you enjoy the holidays?"
"Did you have a nice weekend?"
"How were the roads yesterday on your way home from work?"

4. Reveal a tiny (but not too personal) tidbit about you or your life:

"This has been my best weekend in a long time. I did absolutely nothing!"
"I just returned from a shopping trip to Chicago."
"The first snowfall always makes me feel like a kid again."

5. Ask an easy-to-answer question to encourage your new acquaintance to make a small self-revelation as well:

"What's your favorite holiday?"
"How did you spend the weekend?"
"Which season do you like best?"

Follow many generations of good advice and avoid bringing up politics or religion, especially in early stages of any relationships. Subjects like sports teams or college allegiances can also be too controversial in first encounters. Everyone has favorites. Keep your conversation light and not likely to stir emotions.

These five steps also work well in some situations with people you already know. For example, if you're passing out assignments to your subordinates or students, getting straight to business (*I have a big project for you to work on*) may be too blunt. Requests often go over better in some situations if you foster the trust you need to accomplish something big at work or in school. Spend a few seconds being friendly before dashing into a demand. Take a little time for pleasantries before proceeding to a project.

Example: A sales manager calls a meeting to set record-high sales goals for her staff. Before breaking the news that their monthly quota has been raised to selling 10,000 widgets, she follows the formula for building trust:

1. Start talking about low-risk topics such as the weather or non-controversial news.

   "The first snowfall makes me feel like a kid again. What does winter do to you?

2. Listen actively to responses. Show interest through your face and gestures.

Nod. Smile. Engage. Laugh. Enjoy.

3. Ask questions that draw the group in:

   "Who's going out of town for the holidays?"

4. Reveal a small, but not too personal, fact about yourself.

   "I'm going to downsize my decorations this year!"

5. Ask an easy-to-answer question to encourage some self-revelation from your staff:

   "Are you going to do anything new or different this time?"

A sure sign of people-ability is making time to take an interest in others, regardless of the situation. Showing that you care about others as human beings also builds trust. Don't hurry to your main message. Slip slowly into business at hand. Don't lapse into a lengthy monologue. Just say a few words. Follow the formula for building trust by easing into more serious subjects by asking first:

   "Are you relaxed now and ready to get back to work?"

Listen to replies, then add.

"We need to talk seriously now about an upcoming project."

In a format with familiar faces, such as a co-worker or spouse, you may have fallen into the habit of giving commands without taking time to ensure trust. Being overly direct to your spouse as soon as he or she opens their eyes in the morning usually backfires. Rather than growling, "Take out the trash," start with a few comments that cement your relationship by showing your interest in the other person goes beyond garbage duty:

- "How did you sleep last night?"
- "What do you have planned for today?"
- "Did you remember that it's garbage day?"

Your spouse, your co-worker or your subordinates will be more likely to respond positively if you take the time to acknowledge them as human beings before asking them for help. You may have been delinquent in the past, but it's never too late to work on rebuilding trust.

Many American corporations and institutions have learned the hard way what it takes to earn public trust. Although lying, cheating and unethical behavior top the list of public trust-busters, failing to put people first runs the same risk. That's especially true at traumatic times. Spokespeople for both small and large organizations can build or break public trust depending on how they respond to an emergency, accident or disaster.

Before making comments about a recent school bomb threat, for example, proficient principals put students first. When interviewed, school administrators, corporate leaders and agency representatives with good people skills all should start with something like: "We're glad to report that our school children are safe," or "We want to begin by extending our sympathy to families of the victims."

Remember

- Trust builds relationships and holds them together.
- Building trust takes time. Take time to show interest in others.
- Without trust, there is no real communication or camaraderie.

Rehearse. Practice the 5-step trust-building process with the next person you meet or the next time you get together with someone you already know or make a request of a family member.

Chapter 13

Rebuild Broken Trust

It takes time to put together broken pieces—
and shattered trust.

As any carpenter will tell you, remodeling a house often takes more work than building a new one from the bottom up. In the same way, once severed, trust is more difficult to reconstruct than it was to build from scratch. Repairing damaged relationships can be harder to do than building strong ties from the beginning.

If your landlord, your babysitter or your local plumber loses confidence in you, your word no longer means much. Promises to pay later won't bring repair people back if you're already in arrears with previous bills. It'll take awhile to convince your spouse that you mean what you say if year after year you promise to clean the garage but never seem to get it done. Your husband or wife will see you as untrustworthy when you say you're too busy to help rake the yard, yet you go golfing instead. If there's someone in your life who no longer believes in you, chances are you lost their trust through:

- Broken promises
- All talk and no action
- Saying one thing and doing another
- Telling downright lies

Broken Promises

Just as children remember forever that dad never bought them that pony he promised, friends, family and acquaintances rarely forget a broken vow. You'll never forgive the 16-year-old date who stood you up for the prom, or the best friend who said she'd help you put on a party, but never showed up. You no longer speak to the spouse who committed to loving and obeying you, then didn't live up to those words.

Pledges can be broken in more subtle ways. If you vigorously nod in agreement when everyone in a group is asked to cooperate on a project, then fail to follow through, someone will remember. No matter how casually you declare, "I'll call you soon," then don't bother to pick up the phone, you've lost a shred of someone's confidence in you. If you make, only to break, promises to yourself, you'll even start doubting your own integrity. Unfulfilled personal oaths and exiled New Year's resolutions eventually take a toll on your self-respect.

All Talk—No Action

A supervisor promises raises to employees, then fails to increase their salaries. That's an example of *all talk and no action* at its worst. A 15-year-old keeps telling her mom that she'll clean her room, but doesn't. Her mother gradually loses faith in her honesty. A friend or relative who boasts about a big plan to buy property, start a business or make a fortune—and never actually does it—aptly earns a reputation as a *big talker.*

Empty utterances can be mildly annoying, punch someone directly in the gut or pinch them in the pocketbook. All talk and no action eats away at trust little by little. As promise-makers again and again fail to deliver on what they swear they will do, confidence in them dwindles. Their stories or fantasies may seem innocent on the surface, but eventually no one takes them seriously. Reneging on too many pipe dreams or wasting words on wanna-be wishes creates the illusion that you are untrustworthy, even if you are. Those you share your dreams with never know if you're serious or not.

Saying One Thing, Then Doing Another

A friend says she'll come to your dinner party, but accepts a date for a movie instead. The reason she gives: "My cousin is in town for the evening and wants to see a show." Making excuses is another sure-fire way to set off suspicion that erodes trust. Oft-repeated explanations for canceling or avoiding action take the biggest toll. Everyone's heard them hundreds of times. A few clichés that lead quickly to mistrust include familiar ruses like:

- I'd like to, but I don't have time right now.
- I woke up feeling out of sorts.
- I have a headache.
- My dog ate my homework
- Something unexpected came up that . . .

132

About the third time someone hears excuses like these from the same person, their integrity is seriously in question. On the fourth occasion, trust is likely to be lost.

Downright Dishonesty

Trust quickly quivers when one person in a relationship (husband-wife, supervisor-employee, priest-parishioner, father-child) thinks the other has been dishonest. A boyfriend who shows up late more than once due to car trouble makes his girlfriend wonder if he's being truthful. A teenager who arrives at home after curfew over and over again, providing one excuse or another, causes her parents to question her intentions. A pastor who claims the church is short of money and continues his itinerary for a three-week cruise in the Caribbean makes his parishioners wonder if he's telling the truth about church finances. When facts don't add up, dishonesty is usually the reason.

Ignoring the Best Interests of Others.

Other major relationship-breakers rear their ugly heads in selfishness and self-centeredness. When one person acts without considering another's best interests, trust always wanes. If the boss keeps his staff working right through dinner hour, ignoring their health or their family's welfare, trust in that supervisor weakens. If a spouse spends an entire paycheck on clothing, gambling or alcohol, despite the desire of his partner to pay bills before splurging on frills, trust becomes a major issue between them.

Most people grow suspicious and lose confidence in friends or relatives who seem to use them or outright abuse them. If grown children only talk to their parents when they need extra cash, you're correct to think they're using you as their piggy banks. When a fair-weather friend calls you only when she wants you to watch her children, she's taking advantage of your alliance. The most caring cousin, faithful friend or self-sacrificing sibling will eventually wonder why they're only on someone's radar screen when that person wants something.

Whatever the reason promises are broken or pacts gone kaput, trust can be restored. Reconciliation doesn't always happen, but it is possible in some cases. It's never an easy task. Rebuilding trust takes time and requires determination. Expect to work hard. Here are a few simple steps to start the repair process:

1. Apologize to the person you hurt or disappointed. Be big enough to say to your spouse,

   "I'm truly sorry that I bounced another check."

2. Ask the client you stood up for lunch to forgive your carelessness:

   "Please forgive me for forgetting to meet you for lunch yesterday."

3. Explain your plan for doing better in the future. Suggest another date and time to meet at their convenience. Then show up! Promise to keep better checkbook records. Then, do.

Example:
You missed an important deadline at work.

Apologize:
"I'm sorry I didn't get my project done. Please forgive my delay."

Explain your plan to avoid missing deadlines in the future.
"Next time, I'll plan my time better, or take my work home to finish it."

Follow your plan until you've met at least 10 deadlines. By that time, fulfilling obligations on time will be second nature to you. Your supervisor will likely trust you again. Be aware, also, that you won't be fully trusted with the checkbook again until you write at least 10 checks without bouncing one. To rebuild trust you need to prove your reliability at least 10 times. A single make-up meeting won't mend relationships with friends or lovers immediately. Through research, many marketing departments have come to the conclusion that it takes at least 10 positive actions to override a negative one. To avoid losing customers, businesses take at least 10 steps to bring them back. You'll need to put much more time and energy into reversing a personal relationship where trust has been lost.

If tables are turned and there's someone in your life that you no longer trust—but wish you could, a good way to start reconstructing is to communicate your feelings to that person. Tell your spouse how you feel about blowing the paycheck before paying the bills.

Example:

"I feel scared and insecure when there's not enough money in our account left for rent."

Phrase your feelings or concerns from your perspective. Explain to your supervisor, "I don't feel right about working when my family expects me to be home cooking dinner." Remain quiet and listen while the other person responds to your feelings. You may be disappointed in what he or she has to say. Your boss might try to make excuses like, "We'll all lose our jobs if we don't work overtime." Your spouse could respond by saying something like, "You worry too much." Don't give up easily when you're trying to repair a relationship.

Express your feelings a second time: "I feel uncomfortable living (or working) like this." Then, suggest a solution that will make you feel better about your situation: "I'd feel better if we could try to make changes that would benefit everyone." Wait quietly again for a response.

If necessary, repeat your suggestion once more. On the third strike, you may come to the conclusion that the situation is impossible to fix. Don't allow yourself to be dragged into a debate about who's right and who's wrong. Hopefully, your patient persistence will pay off. In the best-case scenario, you'll get a sincere promise to make some changes in your favor. If nothing happens, you may want to consider making some changes yourself, like looking for another job or accepting the shortcomings of others.

Review

- It takes at least 10 positives to overcome a negative.
- Being dishonest with others is a major trust-buster.
- Apologizing is an important step in rebuilding trust.
- To regain trust, have a plan of action for turning negatives into positives.

Rehearse. Apologize to someone you've lost trust with by failing to follow through on a commitment. Explain how you plan to make sure you will follow through in the future (e.g., "I'll write our coffee dates down and post them on my refrigerator.")

Chapter 14

Mind Your Manners...Monitor Your Character

Do things right . . . do the right thing

For all good people-persons, practicing good manners is a *must.* Learning all you can about social etiquette gives you a plus. Need to brush up on social skills? You can search online anytime for opinions on the subject, or drive to the library and check out books. You'll find many experts, including Miss Manners, Emily Post, Martha Stewart and Ann Landers, who have outlined expectations for behavior. "White gloves for tea" advice may be a bit outdated, but basic good manners are always in style.

After reviewing tips on social customs such as sending and receiving invitations or giving gifts, take time to tackle a few less traditional topics. Google phrases like *21st-century manners,* or *current practices in polite behavior.* Try other related key words. While today's social standards are much more relaxed than those of previous decades, doing things right—and doing the right thing—still matter when it comes to people-ability.

Good social graces can be great assets for getting along with others in most situations, including the all-important job market and business world. Whatever you call it—manners, etiquette or social savvy—using correct social customs and conventions can affect your reputation and your career. Since most people spend more time at work today than they do at home or at high-class social events such as ballets or formal balls, pursuing professional etiquette stands out in the practice of people-ability.

Candidates for top jobs will often be invited to dinner or social events as part of the interview process. Members of the firm want to know in advance if their newly hired executive chews with mouth closed. Employers show interest in who keeps elbows off the table and sits up straight rather than hanging over his bowl of chili or slurping his soup. Work colleagues, as well as friends, neighbors and family members, all appreciate sharing bread with someone who knows and uses basic mealtime manners. Today's standards suggest that we:

- Wait for others to be seated before taking a bite.
- Take small portions and chew with mouth closed.
- Refrain from talking with food in your mouth.
- Slow down and eat at same pace as others at your table.
- Excuse yourself before leaving the table or group.

In the office, at home, or anywhere else in town, good people-persons are also likely to:

- Acknowledge newcomers with introductions.
- Allow everyone to have equal input into conversations.
- Avoid offensive topics, jokes or stories.
- Pass dishes and condiments to everyone at the table.

Many must-observe elements of etiquette that seemed essential in the past, no longer are taken as seriously. Take table manners, for example. In most circles, it's not a notable breach of behavior to start eating salad with the wrong fork or using your soup spoon for dessert. However, a few other flubs at the dining table will still raise eyebrows.

For example, touching every roll before you decide which one to take will be seen as unsavory, as well as unsanitary. It's commonly considered a good idea to let your dessert wait until you've finished your salad and the main meal. Likewise, it's foolish to use your fingers instead of your fork, fail to stifle a burp or sneeze across the table instead of into your inner arm. Good 21st-century etiquette requires common sense more than memorizing strict rules and regulations. A few practical mealtime practices also include:

- Never criticize the food you're served. Keep your opinion to yourself.
- If you don't like sweet potatoes, simply pass them to the next person.
- If there's something on your plate you can't eat, eat around it—without comment.
- Mentally divide foods by number of folks at a table and take only one portion.
- Ask to be excused if you have to leave the group for any reason.

Good table manners go beyond meals. If strangers approach a group of people working together in an office or at a conference table, good people-persons never ignore them. Stand up, introduce yourself and shake hands with each newcomer who joins your group. Ask those already seated around you to take turns introducing themselves—or do it yourself.

Some people learn a wide array of social skills easily at home as they grow up. They can fit comfortably into any situation. Unfortunately, others aren't taught or don't catch on easily. Etiquette deficits put many adults at a disadvantage, especially in the business world. A few simple social skills to take to work with you include:

- Say "please" whenever you make a request.
- Say "thank you" when your request is honored or someone helps you.
- Take turns while talking.
- Listen while others talk.
- Be sensitive to the ideas and feelings of everyone.

More advanced protocol may be required for special occasions, depending on your social circle, workplace or lifestyle. If there's any chance you'll meet a world leader or romp with royalty in the course of your life, the rules become more rigorous. You may have to act, speak or dress according to long-held traditions. Proper procedure might even require you to give greetings in another language, learn the proper way to address a king or know what you should or should not say to a prince or a president.

For the masses and the multitudes in everyday situations, only a few simple rules remain. For most ordinary mortals, manners fall into a few common categories, such as mealtime, meetings, social gatherings and special events. Most modern-day codes of behavior cover wedding etiquette, for example, or how to conduct oneself at a black tie event. Even for those occasions, expectations for behavior vary from group to group. Asking a few questions like, "Do I need to wear a tuxedo?" or "Should I send my gift in advance?" usually covers contemporary conventions.

Some guidelines govern less formal activities, such as parties, discussions or dating. Of course, standing someone up or failing to show up when you've made a date is still considered a fatal faux pas. Popular opinion tells us to behave better than that. All current criteria for good social behavior could be summarized in a few words: *Show respect to other people in everything you say and do.* Nobody curtsies anymore or follows restrictive rules for courting or carrying on conversations. More intricate elements of etiquette, though, are likely to stress appropriate behavior for business meetings, community forums, committee planning sessions. Displaying good business manners mean that all participants:

- Share decision-making in groups of people.
- Negotiate *vs.* insisting on doing things their way.
- Express feelings without becoming aggressive or demanding.
- Discuss areas of conflict calmly.
- Compromise to come to agreement with others.

- Excuse yourself when taking leave of any group.

Practiced and polished people-persons—at work, at home, at school or out in the community—always add personal touches to their etiquette agendas. They are likely to:

- Be supportive of others when they need support.
- Express concern for other people in distress.
- Know when—and when not—to reveal personal information.
- Be thoughtful of others by acknowledging their milestones and accomplishments.

Handshaking when meeting or greeting others continues to be a strong American custom. Everyone needs to know how to do it right. If your grip is too flimsy or you glance away while shaking hands, you're not using the handshake to your advantage. Here are the correct steps.

- Whenever you approach another person or someone introduces you to a third party, immediately extend your arm with an open hand.
- Grasp the other person's hand with enthusiasm, but not so tightly that it hurts.
- Smile and look the other person directly in the eye while saying hello.
- Shake hands firmly, but gently, just two or three times.

Prolonging this gesture makes people look desperate. Avoiding this formality altogether reflects poorly on anyone who doesn't shake hands. Modern-day manners elevate this custom to a staple in our society. Ignore it, and you'll miss a great opportunity to build better relationships.

Along with good manners, good character will always serve you well when dealing with other people. A man or woman of good character is an individual whose actions are honorable. A person of good character is unlikely to do something unethical, immoral or illegal. He or she constantly strives to do what's right. One way to describe good character: *Having the will power to avoid behavior that would embarrass or reflect negatively on you.*

> ***Honesty, integrity and courage are all examples of good character.***

Honesty, integrity and courage also indicate good character. Telling the truth, being true to yourself and having the courage to stand up for what you believe in all earn good marks in people-ability. A person's reputation most often comes from his or her character. Anyone known for lying, cheating, swindling, misleading, or manipulating others settles for stained character. Actions like avoiding responsibility or escaping consequences blemish one's character. So do all attempts to deceive other people. To be of good character, people persons must live all aspects of their lives with integrity.

If you fall short in any of these behaviors, start working to shore up your character immediately. You may want to deny your shortcomings or pass them off as quirks. You might be tempted to hide character blemishes by embellishing the truth or blaming others for your mistakes. It won't work. Just as makeup never completely covers a scar, poor character traits will still be visible below the surface. However innocent character flaws may seem, they can quickly turn into volatile volcanoes if left to smolder. Once ruined, a person's reputation is rarely restored. Once gone, good character is not easy to imitate. Like rebuilding trust, recovering honor can be a long and treacherous journey. Take a look at the following list of traits to decide how much character you have:

Do	**Don't**
Be honest.	Boast or exaggerate the truth to make a good impression.
Be trustworthy.	Fail to follow through on promises you make.
Be true to self.	Be phony or put on airs.
Be ethical.	Set aside your principles just to be popular.
Be moral.	Justify bad behavior because others are doing it.
Be legal.	Break laws just because you think you can get away with it.

Be a cooperative person.	Be a nuisance, a naysayer or a non-stop talker.
Be courteous.	Be argumentative, aggravating or act like a *know-it-all.*
Be courageous.	Have the guts to do what's right!

Rehearse

A. Think of people you know who get along well with other people. List all the traits of character that make those people successful in their relationships.

   1. _____.

   2. _____.

   3. _____.

   4. _____.

   5. _____.

B. List examples of good manners exhibited by someone you admire for their people skills.

   1. _____.

   2. _____.

   3. _____.

   4. _____.

Chapter 15

ABCs of School and Office Interpersonal Skills

People skills make schools and offices more productive places.

The Office . . . or the classroom . . . can be someone's second home—or a snake pit—depending on the interpersonal skills of those who work or study together. If Olga Office Worker or Billie the School Bully await their prey, then pounce on every peer who displeases them, everyone starts to feel walled in, as if they work in a penitentiary or serve time in a prison. Self-appointed saints or suspected sinners who take notes like prison guards add to any unpleasant atmosphere. When someone stands guard to report every move made by colleagues or classmates, they turn their surroundings into junior jailhouses. Bean counters and other persnickety people who make way too much of anyone's mistakes turn workplaces into detention centers and schools into reformatories.

Any place where criticism, unkindness or close scrutiny reigns puts people on edge. Fearful and frustrated, everyone is likely to accomplish less. Employees inhibit good ideas and students stifle their creativity. As early as elementary school, some boys or girls set the scene for their classmates through catty comments. Instead of studying, they seem to wait for every chance they get to ridicule other pupils. Office bullies lurk in hallways or bathrooms to intimidate their associates with their disdainful smirks or callous words. Any school or workplace leader has a choice to accept or prevent such behavior at their sites. Leaders can either cater to the cast of characters who make others shudder, or they can curtail offensive activities. First, school principals and office executives need to recognize bullying and badgering when they see it.

Basic training in people skills can make a difference in any office environment or school climate. If the people in charge don't take the lead to make daily life livable for everyone, someone else should speak up. Talk to your office supervisor or assistant principal about the problem. Ask to discuss *consideration of others* or *anti-bullying strategies* at your next staff meeting. Add those topics to the agenda. To build ownership in ideas to improve the atmosphere, everyone should be involved in setting building-wide standards of behavior. In large organizations, where input from everyone seems impossible, provide a list of 10 or 12 new rules and ask everyone to rank their top four or five.

After getting consensus, post a short list of office standards by drinking fountains, water coolers and copy machines to remind fellow workers to observe workplace norms. Include items such as:

- Treat others as you wish to be treated.
- Pitch in when you're asked for help.
- Share treats, not gossip.

- Put away anything you take out.
- Keep office space neat and clean.

In good schools, every teacher should display a set of classroom rules developed with insights from other staff members, parents and students:

- Show respect to all adults.
- Be kind to your classmates.
- Always do your best work.

Little steps like these go a long way to preserve peace, save sanity and turn treachery and turmoil into tranquility. Interpersonal skills for classrooms or offices should start with this 18-Karat Rule: *Treat fellow students or workers the way you wish they would treat you.* If everyone aboard observed this primary people skill, inhabitants would find workplaces and schoolhouses better places to do business. Performance would improve. People respond according to the conditions under which they work, study or live. Review the following suggestions for applying people skills that will make any office a more professional place:

Be personal, but professional. Be yourself, be open and be friendly in every worksite interaction, but also realize where to draw the line. It's perfectly OK to use first names, for example, but assigning nicknames to people in your office is far too personal. Deciding to call someone Slim or Squirt may be fine for your family and friends, but not so good for co-workers. Laugh and joke with colleagues as long as you don't overstep personal or professional boundaries. Making fun of fellow workers is never funny. Negative references to age, sex, race, religion or national background are not only offensive. Such slurs are also illegal in any setting—school, office or factory floor.

Even though you may spend more hours a day with the person in the next cubicle than you do with your spouse, refrain from getting too close for comfort. Observe the old adage that *familiarity breeds contempt.* Sharing combs, clothing or collateral with colleagues takes the Golden Rule way too far. Expecting colleagues to listen to a litany of personal problems is also off limits. Going on and on about yourself or your family's achievements is another no-no, along with allowing relatives to show up at work—unless it's a special occasion, like take your Daughter to Work day.

You may eventually become good friends with some colleagues, just as classmates tend to do. It's wise, though, to reserve camaraderie for after work hours. Other staff members don't want to feel like their workplace has become a sorority or fraternity for just a few people. Avoid public displays of any special friendships.

Communicate professionally. Good people persons communicate in some way with everyone around them, not just talk to their favorite friends among fellow workers. You should at least nod or smile at everyone you encounter during the course of the day. You don't need to run around acting as an unofficial welcoming committee. However, people will notice if you don't acknowledge their presence. Show a sign of recognition when you come face to face with all other office occupants. If you don't at least smile, you'll look like a snob or earn a reputation as the office crank. Keep your contacts professional, polite and personable.

Avoid using slang or spewing swear words in the office. Even among the best of colleagues, limit your language to professionally accepted words. When commenting on the quality of another person's project, for example, "That's cool" (or hot!) may be acceptable in high schools, but sounds a little juvenile at work. In the office, always use standard English instead of slang. Don't be tempted to punctuate your feelings with foul language. You may think there's no better way to describe your dismay than with a string of expletives. However, someone within earshot will surely find swearing offensive.

Spell-check everything. Stick with standard grammar in writing as well as speech. Reread every sentence you key into your computer to mail or email. Make it a habit to hit the *spell check* option before you push the *send* button. If written or spoken communication is not your best skill, enroll in a refresher course or keep an English language reference book on your desk. More than one career has been sidetracked by inadequate communication, written or spoken.

You represent your company to both outsiders and insiders, so review everything you produce for accuracy, grammar and spelling. If you're still in school, pay close attention to red marks made on your written assignments. The quality of your communication has everything to do with how far you will go in your company and in your career. You'll pay a high price for conjugating verbs incorrectly, using sentences such as "We *was* scared" or "You *was* there."

Keep your volume at a professional level. Use an *inside* voice (the quiet one) from the time you enter your building's interior until the five o'clock whistle blows. Office hours are brain-power hours, especially in the Information Age. If your voice is too loud while talking on the phone or taking care of other business, you're probably breaking someone else's concentration, maybe even preventing them from coming up with their best idea yet.

Leave your personal problems at home. Whispering the latest details of your divorce to your best office buddy is not only impolite to others in range, but it's also out of place. Make a lunch date if you need to spill your story to someone who works with you. It's rude to plan parties or personal weekend retreats in the presence of people who won't be there.

Never talk publicly about private company matters. Subjects such as product design, client problems or customer lists belong to your employer. What happens in your office, like what happens in Las Vegas, should stay there. When you need to discuss issues that aren't meant for public consumption, request private meetings with supervisors or co-workers. Never try to communicate concerns or correct people while other employees, customers, clients, students or guests can hear you.

Do your part to make things run smoothly. When it comes to teamwork and/or cooperation, follow best practices like these:

- Disagree without being disagreeable.
- Lead or follow, whichever a situation requires.
- Work to solve problems, not create them.
- Align your goals with group goals and organizational objectives.
- Let the majority rule.
- Cooperate with others.
- Be able to work with people of all backgrounds, cultures and beliefs.

The number one reason employees run into problems at work is that they can't get along with their fellow workers. Team work takes people-ability at its most professional levels.

Confirm and affirm everything. The most successful 21st-century citizens always confirm appointments or meetings. With today's technology, it's easy to ensure that plans materialize. Call, leave a voice mail message, or send an email to confirm the date, time and place before each business meeting you've scheduled. Confirmation reduces the likelihood for disappointment. Even in friendships, it's far better to jolt someone's memory than to pout later when he or she disappoints you. Don't hesitate to remind your supervisor—at least 24 hours in advance—that it's time to keep that scheduled meeting to discuss your annual raise. A short email will do. You're more likely to snag something when you remind them of your mission or provide advance notice.

Exercise office etiquette. Your co-workers and supervisors may not be your best friends, but you'll be pegged as the enemy if you lack simple social etiquette expected in the office. Acts like ignoring invitations to socialize with colleagues, or skipping your turn to bring a treat annoy others. If you sit alone every day at your desk for lunch while everyone else congregates in the cafeteria, you're likely to generate angst. A few tips for office etiquette:

- Join the crowd and go out to lunch occasionally—and follow suit for paying the bill.
- Participate in office parties and picnics no matter how much you may hate them.
- Circulate. Acknowledge everyone you work with at all social events.
- Arrive at the office clean, combed and odor-free, but go easy on the cologne.
- Cover your mouth when you cough or sneeze.
- Stay home when you're really sick to avoid infecting others.
- Treat all fellow workers the same, no matter what job title they hold.

- Never take credit for someone else's work.
- Don't try to dump your work on unsuspecting co-workers.
- Take your eyes off your computer screen when a colleague asks you a question.
- Don't answer your cell phone in mid-conversation. Keep sound off at work.
- Never tell jokes about race, gender, age, disabilities, sexual orientation or religion.

If you're not guilty of such bad behaviors, but a few fellow workers are, gently remind them not to be rude. Use first person or "I" sentences rather than second person or "You" sentences. Admit: "I don't like jokes that mock people," vs. preaching with statements like "You shouldn't tell jokes that make fun of people."

Rethink: Recall an incident in your office or workplace where you may have previously acted unprofessionally. Record below how you will apply people-ability to this situation in the future:

Chapter 16

People Skills for Supervisors and Managers

Leaders carry the ball for creating good interpersonal atmospheres.

Company leaders carry the ball for creating work climates that encourage good interpersonal relations. If managers set the pace for practicing people skills, employees usually imitate their behavior. If the boss brings in the first bag of donuts, others will follow suit. Several steps good supervisors can take to foster people skills among their staff include:

- Communicate that you care about people.
- Use as a motto such as: "When everyone works together; everyone wins."
- Let each employee know often that their work counts and they are needed.
- Stress teamwork from the first employment interview of all new people.
- Push collaboration at department meetings, lunches or events.
- Practice listening carefully—while keeping your mouth shut!

Remember the R&R theory of management: Reward and Recognition. Everyone likes praise and most people are motivated by rewards. Superior supervisors add a third

R—Responsibility—to their repertoire of people-ability. Here are some examples of the R & R & R method in action.

Responsibility

- Give each employee at least one responsibility for making the office atmosphere pleasant and people-oriented (e.g., decorate the office, plan a meeting, take reservations for the company picnic, birthday celebrations, flower fund).
- Provide a small budget for each department head to purchase personal incidentals for workplace use (coffee, paper cups, cards or flowers to celebrate special occasions, etc.).
- Give employees choices in training and education opportunities, perhaps even in benefits.
- Allow employees to choose their own break times or lunch hours if possible.
- Ask each staff member to turn in a list of their accomplishments occasionally.
- Assign existing staff as mentors to new employees.

Recognition

- Encourage employees to post all thank-you notes from customers.
- Provide a bulletin board for staff to display news articles or photos of their families.
- Personally thank people for a job well done or send them thank-you notes.

- Write and publish features or stories on employee contributions in the company newsletter.
- Create a "Hall of Fame" where employees are recognized for significant contributions.
- Follow up with a thank-you note from the CEO to the family of the "Hall of Fame" inductee.

Reward

- Celebrate the completion of big office projects with a pizza party or catered lunch.
- Award gift cards or certificates to Employees of the Month (nominated by peers).
- Recognize teams that reach goals with a traveling trophy each month.
- If funds are tight, reward with double lunch breaks or late morning workday starts.
- Publicly compliment your staff often.

What are the two most effective words managers can use in promoting people-ability and motivating people? Most human resource managers agree on *Thank you!* All too often, supervisors see their role as simply making sure everyone in the office or on the factory floor is doing their work.

In the bigger picture, the purpose of managers and supervisors may be to motivate people to do their work *well*. Since motivation comes from within, not from someone else, savvy supervisors stay on the lookout for ways to bring out motivation in people. Here are a few basic steps leaders can take to develop dynamic teams, departments or corporations:

- Strive for total clarity in giving directions or instructions.
- Set the stage by providing support and materials needed for every job.
- Develop pride and competence through personal career development.
- Set a course of action with goals and strategies for each project.
- Make all expected outcomes clear.
- Excite people with new ideas for recognition and rewards.
- Increase individual self-worth through responsibility and trust.
- Seek input from staff to build ownership.
- Show interest in individual and group progress.
- Show appreciation—say thank you often.

And finally, stay ahead of the issues. Anticipate problems and step in with prevention or intervention.

Rehearse.

1. Anticipate problems in your staff's next project. Develop a three-point plan to prevent potential problems and a three-point plan to intervene if problems occur.
2. Write a thank-you note to an employee who has gone beyond the call of duty.

Chapter 17

Good People Skills = Good Customer Service

Treating customers well is wise for your wallet and corporate bottom line.

Is the customer really always right? If you want to keep your job, keep in mind that the customer is king. King or queen, prince, pauper or crackpot, your customer can go to a different company for the same product or pick a competitor to deliver the service he or she needs. The high cost of poor people-ability in business becomes apparent in sluggish sales, falling profits, lots of layoffs, loss of jobs, even company closings. That's why so many HR managers search for people skills and expect job candidates to be able to describe them. When a customer comes in with a complaint, a good people person always makes him feel that his position is understood.

Example:

Mr. X returns a pair of pants his wife bought him for his birthday. He claims that the quality of the cloth isn't up to par.

A sales clerk with good interpersonal skills immediately apologizes, saying something Like, "I'm sorry you're not satisfied, Mr. X." Then, she shows him other brands of slacks that might better meet his standards. At all costs, she avoids challenging his opinion.

Employees with people-ability know enough to allow customers to be right—even when they're wrong! You don't have to agree with another person's opinion. You might not believe they're telling the truth about product quality or poor service. Customer complaints may be the worse part of your job, but to practice people-ability with clients or customers, you've got to hear them out. There's no other way to handle a disgruntled individual.

Consider the case of Mr. X. He's satisfied with his new trousers, and the store where his wife bought them keeps a customer. Everyone's still in business. The clerk doesn't have to worry about being laid off. Probably no one would have to fear losing their jobs, if all clerks let Mr. Y or Ms. Z make their cases, while listening courteously to them. If Mr. Y claims he was overcharged, listen to him.

Example:

Mr. Y insists that the handbag he bought his wife was on sale at half-price the day he made the purchase. He explains that he noticed that he was charged the regular price only after he arrived at home yesterday.

Possessing people-ability, the salesperson politely listens to Mr. Y's story. She empathizes with her customer's situation, acknowledging how disappointed he must have felt.

Then, the salesperson shows Mr. Y the original ad or sign that clearly states the sale ended several days ago. If the store employee has been empowered to make adjustments, she offers Mr. Y a small discount. If she isn't authorized to do that, she immediately shows Mr. Y comparable products at lower prices. Mr. Y exchanges the purse that wasn't on sale for a similar one that costs much less. He leaves the store in a good mood.

If all employees were trained better in the art of making customer adjustments, more stores would see higher sales figures. Marketing professionals say that it's seven times *more difficult* and *more expensive* to bring in new customers than satisfying current ones.

It's a perk for salespeople to be provided with customer service training. Their earnings are often based on their sales percentages, so it's economically smart. Ambitious store clerks or sales representatives seek out their own lessons in people-ability even if their employer doesn't provide any. Here's what every person working in the field of commerce should know:

- Work hard to make sure your customers choose you.
- Always be courteous and polite—even if they're not!

- Let each customer know that you are grateful for their business.
- Thank your customers or clients often.

If your job—or your salary—depends on your level of customer service, here are a dozen more ways to raise the bar:

1. Treat all customers as if they make it possible for you to receive a paycheck. They do.
2. Greet all customers professionally and with a pleasant voice—in person or by phone.
3. Answer every phone call no later than the third ring.
4. Transfer calls that require extra assistance to appropriate people immediately.
5. Let the customer know how to leave a message if a transfer call isn't answered.
6. Return every phone call as soon as possible, never later than two business days.
7. Respond to questions or concerns within 24 hours.
8. Always ask the customer when a return call will be most convenient.
9. Set up appointments within three days or less, unless there are unusual circumstances.
10. Never make a customer wait more than five minutes—five seconds for an appointment.
11. If there is an emergency that extends the customer's wait time, let the customer know.
12. Maintain confidentiality for all customers.

What you say and how you say it to customers also can affect your own wallet as well as your company's bottom line. Deadly words or phrases to avoid include:

"I can't . . ."
"Yes, but . . ."
"That's our policy."

Hiding behind policy turns off customers. No matter what company SOPs say, offer help in trying to solve a problem, making an exchange or taking a return. Phrases such as "We can't do anything about that" convey to a customer that he's just another peg in the board. Worse yet are clerks or managers who make excuses. Brushing off a customer with phrases like, "We're really busy right now" really says: "We don't have time for you." When an employee complains to a customer that everyone in the company is under too much pressure to take care of your problem now, what he or she really relays is, "You're lower on the totem pole than our bigger clients." The *too busy* disclaimer encourages customers to look elsewhere for products and services. In all encounters with customers, or any other folks for that matter, avoid using the word *but* (use *and* instead). "But" acts like an eraser. It nullifies the value of what you previously said.

Examples.

1. You explain to a customer that you'd really like to help, *but* now is not a good time.

165

2. You admit that you see the customer's point, *but* you're powerless to do anything.

3. You say you understand the client's problem, *but* you can't come up with a solution.

You're much better off saying, "I'll see what I can do to change this." Then, follow through. Anyone who wants to think of himself as an entrepreneur—or a good people person—never utters the words, "I can't."

Granted, some customers are harder to handle than others. Some are angry, unreasonable, or even belligerent. You may feel bullied by some consumers, even threatened. The key to dealing with difficult people is not letting yourself get caught up in their emotions. No matter how loud, bold or boisterous a disgruntled client may be, you must remain calm.

To defuse hostile or furious outbursts, offer the ultimate in customer service. Cater to angry individuals. Wait on them. Offer them coffee or water. Find them a pleasant place to sit down to discuss their issue. Act civilly towards them until they calm down. Copying their crazy behavior will only infuriate them further.

If an uninformed customer comes back to complain about an imaginary oversight or mistake, always apologize: "Oh, we should have told you that" (even if it was clearly printed on the coupon) or "We're so sorry that offer has expired." It won't hurt you and it will help your situation immensely. For sake of apologizing (even if the customer was at fault) be prepared with a rabbit to pull from your hat. Keep consolation prizes in mind for such occasions. You may be able to offer a discount or provide a more current coupon. Always end the transaction by thanking the customer for stopping in.

Some determined people will try to get their way by overwhelming you with their knowledge. For example, they may try to return an opened-and/or-used item by pointing out state law, company policy or best practice. Don't argue with them. There's always a chance they are right. Instead, ask them for help in citing the law, so you'll be better prepared to clear up mistakes. You may be surprised when they return with a photocopy from a law book or a newsletter from their representative.

Let big talkers take action rather than just talk. Send them to an onsite office to enlighten your managers as well. Wouldn't everyone on staff want to know? Suggest that the customer explains his experience to higher authorities to make sure it won't happen again. Tell such well-armed and well-informed customers that you will be glad to make an exchange once your supervisor hears his story and approves the deal.

Further tips on handling tough customers:

- Use "I" statements *vs.* "You" statements. Telling customers how you feel reduces their defensiveness,

Susan K. Maciak

a reaction to perceived criticism when you use "You." Say things like: "I understand. I see your point. I can't agree."

- Ask the customer to help identify areas you both agree on.
- Ask questions to show you want to understand how the customer feels.
- Allow the customer to express their feelings and acknowledge them.
- Describe or repeat what you thought you heard the customer say.
- Address the customer's need for satisfaction, not the solution.
- Find out what motivates the customer and offer alternative solutions. (*What would be a happy ending for you? What if we were able to . . .*)
- Admit error—Claim your blame and others are more likely to admit theirs.

If you're unsuccessful in resolving a customer service problem after trying these techniques, admit defeat and refer the customer to someone else who may be able to help: "Pat Johnson is the real expert on that subject. Let me transfer you to her."

Preventive medicine proves to be the best remedy for dealing with customer complaints. One way to stay ahead of product problems or costly predicaments is through strategic planning. Company leaders to counter clerks can

168

anticipate potential problems and solutions by using the RACE formula in their business practices:

1. **Research—Find out exactly what your customers want and are willing to pay for:**
   Seek input, survey customers, study demographics, etc.
2. **Analyze—Look at the information you gathered and apply it to your situation:**
   Sell the right products and the right package at the right price. Be willing to bargain.
3. **Communicate—Let your customers know about important company policies.**
   Inform customers via messages on labels, packages, signs, brochures, ads, notices.
4. **Evaluate—Find out what works and why it works.**
   Keep records of customer satisfaction. Ask if you can quote happy customers in ads or on your webpage. Post positive feedback on bulletin boards or posters.

It pays to stay in touch with current customers or clients. Keep a pulse on their preferences by requesting their opinions on products or services they purchased. Tuck a customer satisfaction survey in postcard form into every packaged order. Try some old tricks like putting a suggestion box where people can easily put in a few words of advice for better customer service. Attach a pen and leave sticky notes next to the box.

Remember:

- Customers make your paycheck possible, so treat them with special care.
- Preventive medicine in customer services means knowing in advance what your customers want.
- Stay in touch with customers. Conduct surveys. Ask for feedback. Take suggestions.

Chapter 18

Use People Skills to Play the Networking Game

What is the networking game and why should you play it? Networking is nothing more than getting to know lots of people. Practicing people-ability makes networking a cinch—and helps develop skilled players in this game. In short, everyone needs to network to get ahead in today's world. *What you know* trumps *who you know* in the Age of Technology. However, the people you know still open doors and align themselves as allies. All you need to do to network is to approach other people and start talking to them. Conversation starters include:

- What's your favorite way to spend a rainy afternoon like today?
- If you could go on vacation anywhere in the world, where would you go? Why?
- Who's had the most influence on your life? How?

Most of us know the benefits of networking. Many of us find it hard to do. We feel uncomfortable going out of our way to make new friends, especially when we have an ulterior motive like building a foundation of folks who will help support us. Those we know best make us most comfortable, but probably already watch out for us. Expanding our network often puts us in uncomfortable positions or places.

Whether your base will be built with business associates, colleagues, relatives, friends, neighbors or strangers, the point of the networking game is the same. Networking is nothing more than building new relationships. You play the game by lining up people you can count on. Your network includes anyone who is open to letting you contact them for information, opinions or advice. Most folks are flattered to be called on for their expertise. If your relationship flourishes, you may be able to request mentoring, job recommendations or references from some people in your network. To do that, you need to nourish your relationships. Make it a point to get in touch with old and new friends from time to time.

As several popular singers once sang, "People need people." To get ahead in today's world, you need to network with many other people. A good networker keeps hundreds of business cards. Even if you break out in hives at the thought of approaching strangers, it's critical to be a confident networker who can connect with others. In today's tough world, you can't go it alone. You need to collaborate with other people to:

- Keep up with today's explosion of ever-increasing knowledge.
- Learn how to decide on and use ever-advancing technology.
- Stay abreast of important issues in your industry.
- Build your client or customer base.

A strong network also helps when you:

- Need job leads or references.
- Want to be elected to public office.
- Hope to be promoted to the next level in your company.
- Would like a network of neighbors for home emergencies.

In the past, when most of us lived and worked in much smaller communities, everyone nearby was automatically in our network. Those were the days when you could break into a conversation on your 4-way party line to report a fire, or count on friends and neighbors to help raise your barn. In the 21st century, neighbors are not as easily available. Some prefer not to be accessible. You need to build your own network for support.

Is networking an art or a science? It can be both. Networking combines the science of human behavior with the art of communications some might say. Networking takes understanding human nature and knowing how to form relationships. It involves many of the people skills previously presented in this book. Art or science, networking has become an essential strategy for advancing in careers and creating caring communities. It can be career-oriented—or carried on closer to home. Your network can include neighbors, family members, friends, co-workers, club members, fellow church members or community leaders. Your peers can be among your most powerful allies or you can learn from today's youth or lean on the older generation for assistance. Networking is simply building lasting relationships with people of any age.

The *reach-out-and-touch-someone nature* of networking is crucial in today's high-tech environment. Human connections enhanced through networking have become like strings that bind us all together in the maze of wireless phones and Internet access, double-wide fiber optic cables and fist-sized computers. Social networks like Facebook or Twitter bestow us with big link-building bonuses. Face-to-face networking works even better. Go out of your way to meet new people. Network at meetings, at parties, at special events. Network in the post office or at the grocery store. Any place where people gather can be your turn to play the networking game.

Many of us followed this phenomenon long before the first cell phone delivered an email or allowed text messaging and photo sharing. Most of us have been building relationships all of our lives. As five-year-old wallflowers in kindergarten, we pushed ourselves to pick a few playmates. At 10, we sought out classmates who would trade snacks with us. As 15-year-olds, we joined the basketball team, the journalism staff or the drama club to get to know other teens. Some of the best connections consist of people who have the same interests as ours.

Any sort of human bond we make—from flirting to floating ideas off friends—all add up to networking. Common experiences lead to friendships. Proximity to people provides enough incentive for interaction. That's all networking really is—building relationships. Another way to define networking is *spreading our wings to make new friends in new places.*

Recently launched web sites, like Linked-In or Twitter, make it possible to network with anyone anywhere in the world. To make friends or search for supporters as far away as Australia, China or Africa, all you need to do is log onto your computer. But step back in time a few years to look at some of the more traditional networking venues. Networking can take place almost anywhere:

- At work
- At school
- At church
- In the community
- In the neighborhood
- In groups, clubs and organizations
- At events, such as weddings, graduations or celebrations
- Even at malls, grocery stores and other public places

It's easier to get to know people in these places than you may think. Most relationships simply start with a smile. A friendly face makes you more approachable. Give yourself a happy look and others will respond more favorably to you. Think back at all your relationships that began with a grin:

- Your lifelong friendships
- Your first date
- Your marriage

All you need to network is a smile and the courage to break out of your comfort zone. Don't wait until you're desperate to start building a network of people to fall back on. Start now. It could take years to develop a dependable network. Make a conscious effort to form friendships today.

> **Show interest and enthusiasm while being a good listener.**

Build your network person by person. Start by introducing yourself to someone new wherever you are. It helps if you know exactly what you're going to say. In other words, prepare a pitch. Start with your name. Set yourself apart from the crowd with a short statement that defines you. Then, turn your attention to the other person.

Example:
- Smile and introduce yourself.
- Explain your connection to the event. *(I'm the bride's cousin* or *I'm a business owner here to learn more about marketing—*or whatever brought you here).
- Show your interest in the other person. (*And what brings you here today?*)

From that simple introduction, conversation will flow naturally:

- Where are you from?
- How far is that from here?
- Where do you work?

Show interest and enthusiasm while being a good listener. A stranger will quickly grow into a friend.

To nail down professional relationships, offer your business card or provide your phone number or email address to associates you meet. Ask for theirs. Then, tell your new acquaintance, "If there's anything I can do to help you, don't hesitate to contact me."

The most solid way to cinch a networking deal is to offer to help others first. Good networkers make it a point to follow up every contact immediately to continue conversation. It's important to stay in touch with everyone in your network at least once a year. If you make just one or two phone calls a year to everyone in your network, you won't be forgotten. If you offer to help each contact solve a problem, you'll get their attention. Sending holiday cards is one way to maintain relationships of all kinds. With today's technology, staying in touch can be even easier than ever with a quick email reminder that you're available if those in your network need help or advice.

Remember

- The point of networking is to build relationships with people you can call on later.
- Common experiences and communications build relationships.
- The best way to cinch a networking deal is by offering to help or support others first.

Rehearse. If networking scares you, practice first in safe places—while waiting in line at your local grocery store, for example. Tap the shoulder of the person in front of you. Smile. Introduce yourself. Explain what you're doing in the store: "I just dropped in for a gallon of milk." Ask the other person something light like: "And what brings you to Top Notch grocery store today?" See where the conversation goes.

Chapter 19

Ace an Interview ... with Perfect People Skills

Don't act like a robot. You could be replaced with one!

In the process of any job search, you'll be called in for an interview. If you do your homework, you'll research the company that may be interested in you, write down date, place, time and names of people you'll meet and get directions to the interview site. You'll dress professionally, anticipate questions you'll be asked and leave your house early enough to arrive on time. Once you knock on the door, though, your people skills will carry the day. You'll need to display your best interpersonal behavior from the first person you meet to the last.

To apply great people skills while going through your interview, follow this formula:

- Smile.
- Be friendly to everyone, including receptionists and office assistants.
- Reach out to shake hands to everyone you meet.
- Smile and maintain eye contact while shaking hands.
- Repeat each new person's name as you say hello (Hello, Justin—or Hello, Jane).
- Ask: "Where would you like me to sit?"

- Sit up straight, but relaxed, with hands (not elbows) on table.
- Thank interviewers for giving you this opportunity.
- Let interviewers take the lead from there.
- Make eye contact with everyone at table while answering questions.

Some interview questions are carefully calculated to test your people skills. If not handled in the right way, those queries can become sand traps. Topping all problem questions are traditional probes, such as "Tell me about yourself" or "What makes you the person you are?"

Job candidates who begin at their birth and expound exponentially get off to a bad start. Any other lengthy dissertations are just as dangerous. Answers should be limited to two or three statements, even when it comes to summaries of your life experience. It's wise to limit your responses to bare essentials.

Which details of your life are most likely to lead you to getting the job? Choose brief comments about each. You may want to mention:

1. I've always been a leader since my days as quarterback (or first chair orchestra)
2. I worked my way through State University and graduated on time.
3. I've been interested in accounting since opening my first checking account.

In three short sentences like these, you've hit all the bases—the ones related to your qualifications for the job. That's all you need to offer. Your interviewers will ask you enough questions to pull out more detail as needed. If they follow up with a general question like, "What else can you tell us about yourself," have two or three more job-related statements ready.

Interviewers will often leave lulls in the conversation just to see if candidates will try to load them with unsolicited information. Don't be tempted to fill in the gaps. It's during quiet moments like these that most job candidates say something self-incriminating that leads to a lost job opportunity. Use focused listening instead. Try to talk less than 30 percent of the time.

No matter how eloquently you described your people skills in your résumé, if you slip in negative things in an interview about past employers, supervisors or fellow workers, you're also in trouble. Your lack of respect for others will be apparent to everyone immediately. Other tip-offs that you lack people-ability while interviewing for a job include:

- Arriving at an interview dressed for a dance or day at the beach vs. business.
- Awkward, weak or non-existent handshakes—before or after interviewing.
- Slouching in your seat rather than leaning forward to show interest.

- Chewing gum or sucking on a cough drop during the interview.
- Leaving your cell phone on only to have it ring while you're interviewing.
- Answering your cell phone while interviewing. (It's been done!).
- Failing to show interest in the interviewers or the job they have to offer.
- Emphasizing pay, work hours or benefits vs. what you can do for others.
- Knowing nothing about the company that is interviewing you for a job.
- Leaving an interview without asking any questions about the job or company.
- Failing to thank interviewers for their time.
- Forgetting to send thank you notes in addition to verbally thanking them.

Human resource managers, or the people who interview and hire, are on the lookout for red flags. Signaling trouble to them are job candidates who complain about past employers, or unemployed individuals who blame someone else for their bad luck. A candidate's lack of social skills can cause potential employers to wonder: "What kind of impression would this candidate make on our customers?"

Just one or two lapses in basic courtesies bring out concerns. Likewise, fidgeting, such as tapping on the table, pulling on a strand of hair or showing other idiosyncrasies can sabotage your job search, no matter how remarkable your credentials may be.

As you learned in an earlier chapter, what you wear to the interview also says more than many of your answers to interview questions. Before you open your mouth, your attire gives away your attitude. How you appear shows in an instant how much or how little you respect the interview process and people conducting it. If you show up in wrinkled or worn-out clothing, for example, or have dirty, disheveled hair, you reveal lack of respect for yourself and others. You demonstrate severely damaged people-ability. Looking like you mean business lets people know more about your qualifications than degrees or diplomas do.

To test your acumen when it comes to interview attire, take this quiz on business and professional appearance. Check each of your answers before moving on to the next question.

QUIZ. Dress Code for Job Interviews

Mark T for true, F for false. Then, check your answer immediately.

1. ___ **Dark pants or skirt with a white shirt or blouse make good choices for job interviews or other professional encounters.**

TRUE. White shirts present a clean image, important for first impressions. Dark pants/skirts look more businesslike than other colors. Complete your look with a dark jacket or sweater for extra professional points.

2. ____ It's a good idea to try on clothing in advance to make sure you feel comfortable.

TRUE. You'll feel more comfortable at an interview or at an important meeting if you know your clothes fit right and look right. You'll make others squirm, too, with ill-fitting outfits.

4. ____ Any color nail polish is acceptable to wear to job interviews or to work.

FALSE. Well-manicured nails with clear polish make the best impression. Customers and co-workers alike see outlandish-colored nails as inappropriate in a business setting.

5. ____ No one will notice what kind of shoes you wear to work or a job interview.

FALSE: Look well-groomed from head to toe. Scuffed or scruffy shoes make you appear unpolished. Your appearance could reflect on your professionalism or hurt the whole team.

6. ___ **Athletic or gym shoes are OK for an interview if they match your clothes.**

FALSE. Only dress shoes should be worn to job interviews. Avoid sandals or gym shoes of any kind.

7. ___ **Navy blue is the best color to wear to work if you hope to be promoted some day or want to advance in the company.**

TRUE. Navy blue is a traditional and respected color. It's worn by leaders and it commands respect. Studies show that people who wear navy are taken more seriously by others.

8. ___ **Perfume or cologne is considered a must to wear to an interview and on the job.**

FALSE. Perfume or cologne should be used sparingly. Others may dislike it or associate it with a negative. Never try to disguise body odor with artificial aromas. Take a bath and wash your hair before an interview (or before going to work) instead. More than one career has been sabotaged by careless grooming.

9. ___ **"Professional" means to look, sound and act like you take your job seriously.**

TRUE. To have a commanding presence in the workplace, always look good, speak clearly and considerately and take your job seriously.

10. ___ To look classy, wear lots of jewelry to work, meetings or job interviews.

FALSE. Three pieces of conservative jewelry (including rings) add up to the maximum. Also, remove any unusual body piercing.

11. ___ Business clothing consists of whatever is in style or what everyone else wears.

FALSE. Conservative basics like jackets, slacks or skirts and dress suits are best for everyone.

12. ___ Know your company's dress policy—and follow it—if you want to succeed.

TRUE: You represent your company and your co-workers. Dress to make them proud of you. You won't be successful in your career goals unless you can follow both written and unwritten dress codes for work.

Both written and unwritten dress codes, along with people skills covered in this book, are essential pieces in getting picked, or hired, for a job. Practice perfect people-ability and you will make a good impression—and ace your interview!

Remember

- If you claim good people skills in your résumé, show potential employers you practice them.
- Lack of eye contact and awkward handshakes are perceived as poor people skills.
- What you wear to a job interview speaks louder than your answers to some questions.

Chapter 20

People Problems and Practical Solutions

Practicing good people skills may take overcoming obstacles.

Life is never without problems, and neither are human relationships. Friendships, marriages, families, church groups, clubs, classrooms and communities all fall victim to human error from time to time. Offices, firms and factory floors feature misunderstandings, mistrust and miscommunications regularly. When communication breaks down and relationships go astray, good people persons always analyze each situation, change strategies or develop new ones. Some attempts to improve people-ability may leave you wondering whether it's worth the effort, but without trying, small blips can turn into big botches or bungles.

Before things are blown completely out of proportion, it's a good idea to rethink issues and seek possible solutions. Disagreement over land use or zoning can be counted on to cause community discontent. Family money issues or discipline of children can become culprits that end in chaos in homes. A single word taken out of context can ignite a small fire that soon becomes a raging inferno in schools, churches or offices. Classroom clashes, neighborhood tiffs and family feuds are all troublesome events that require intervention before turning into emergencies. Here are a few general pointers for people persons who want to prevent an all-out five-alarm fire:

- Ask those involved to describe the problem from each point of view (pro and con).
- Pause before responding (to show you heard what was said).
- Be direct, but don't take a position—deal with a need.
- State your case calmly and accurately.

When responding to volatile situations, say something like, "It looks like we need to compromise on the right punishment for our kids when they talk back to us" or "We need to know the majority opinion on where commercial zoning should be available in our community."

Once everyone knows what needs to be done to resolve a divided issue, good people persons ask for ideas on how to compromise, whether on matters of discipline, the community's preferences for zoning or any other matter. You don't have to be the person in charge to do this. Any good people person can take the lead in situations like these.

Sometimes a problem involves us personally or a friend who is seeking our advice. In that case, we need to rethink the situation or write down the facts before analyzing them and dealing with needs that are not being met.

SAMPLE SCENARIO: Sara and Mark

Sara complains to her friend that she and her husband, Mark, don't communicate anymore.

> "The only thing he says to me these days is what he wants for dinner," she claims. "Or that he'll be home late tomorrow. I want us to share our dreams and goals again, the way we did when we were dating—not just talk about our daily routines."

Sara admits that she hasn't mentioned to Mark what she'd rather discuss. Instead, she pouts:

> "If I have to tell him what to say, it doesn't mean much."

Sara's friend responds:

> "Well, what topics do you talk to Mark about?"

Sara thinks before answering:

> "I try to tell him about my day at work, but he walks away before I finish describing all the details."

Unmet "needs" to ponder: What needs are not being communicated in this relationship?

1. What expectations does Sara need to convey to Mark?
2. What does Mark need from Sara that she's not providing?
3. How can this couple come to agreement on each other's needs?

What's wrong with this relationship? Sara's friend slyly stumbles on the answer to Sara's dilemma with the questions she poses. Sara confides in her friend, rather than telling Mark, that she would rather share dreams and goals with her husband than talk about daily chores.

Yet, when she starts a conversation with him, what does she open with? A diatribe of daily details from her workplace! In other words, she talks about daily chores, exactly what she says Mark does. Mark makes a mistake by walking away while she's still talking, but other topics could have kept him listening longer. Dale Carnegie would say, "The royal road to a man's heart is to talk to him about the things he treasures most."

If misunderstandings are one-to-one or more personal than problems that arise in larger groups, consider adding these pointers to the basic rules for building understanding by considering others' needs:

- Persuade with facts, not force.
- Use "I" statements to reduce defensiveness.

Rather than trying to force other people to meet your needs, provide a few facts about yourself that justify your need to discuss dreams, rather than humdrum routine:

> "I like to escape from day-to-day drudgery by discussing future dreams."
>
> "I want you to be a part of my goals and dreams."

Don't ruin the chance to repair this relationship by placing blame ("It's your fault, because you always walk away when I'm talking.").

- Accept blame when you're at fault.
- Let the other person save face.
- Avoid adding "but" to any phrase ("I will, but not right now").
- Be fair—even in an argument. (No name-calling, sarcasm or ridicule).

All relationships suffer when we start treating those closest to us in ways we wouldn't want to be treated. Apply the Golden Rule.

There are as many answers as there are questions, as many solutions as there are problems when practicing people-ability. You don't have to be a genius to be a genuine people person. All it takes is common sense—and consideration of others. Here are some situations commonly encountered by individuals struggling to become better people persons.

Other Problems and Solutions

Problem. "I strive to be a good people person, but often find that others take advantage of me because I'm too nice. How can I practice people-ability and not be a pushover?"

Solution. You don't have to be a martyr to be a good people person. People-ability doesn't mean doing someone else's work or taking on responsibilities that aren't yours. It doesn't mean you have to bow to peer pressure, or allow yourself to be manipulated by others. People-ability means treating everyone with respect. You can treat others kindly without letting them take advantage of you. If you are going too far to please others, you may need to practice assertiveness.

Three Steps to Assertiveness:
1. State your position. Stick to it. *I understand you need help, but all I can give you is advice.*
2. Repeat without reasons or excuses. *The best thing I can offer you right now is advice.*
3. Put subtle pressure on the other person. *You're smart enough to finish that project on your own. You'll feel good about doing the work yourself.*

Problem. "I'm worried that being too friendly with my staff will sabotage our supervisor-employee relationship."

Solution. It will—only if you go overboard and try to become best friends with everyone. Being friendly or showing interest in someone is not the same as becoming their bosom buddy. Keep your encounters with others brief and professional, but friendly. Show interest in people as human beings.

Problem. "Are there any rules for people-ability when it comes to sending email?"

Solution. The first rule for email is to *think* before you click *send.* It's so easy to be misunderstood with this new form of communication. Good food for thought when composing emails: Say to others only what you would want them to say to you. Hastily crafted messages emailed in moments of anger or frustration too often cause bigger problems, breakdowns in trust and plenty of regret.

Problem. "Does it show poor people skills to keep your office door closed?"

Solution. It's OK to close your office doors occasionally for a variety of reasons, including critical deadlines, conference calls and confidential discussions. But supervisors or any other employees who keep their doors shut all the time risk earning a reputation as a not-so-good people person. A constantly closed entrance signals that you don't want to be bothered by other people—ever. If you need privacy for a good reason, post a sign on your door telling when you'll be available to see others again.

Problem. "My job requires me to deal with anger on a regular basis. How can I become a better people person under such circumstances?"

Solution. Anger is an emotion that everyone experiences at times, some people more than others. In an outburst, adrenalin is released for a few minutes, taking the angry person to a high state, followed by a low state. To cope with the anger of others, it helps to know that this emotional release is often a survival strategy. However, anger can be defused by a knowledgeable people person. Try these techniques:

- Stand next to an angry person (not across from him or her).
- Allow for anger reduction time (12 to 20 minutes to complete the adrenaline rush).
- Don't argue (just listen at first to the outburst).
- Acknowledge feelings (I understand how you feel).
- Use "I" statements (I see that you're upset).
- Get them alone, if possible (Let's go somewhere quiet and talk about this).
- Listen to their side of the story (Tell me what happened to make you so mad).

Remain calm, acknowledge anger and listen carefully to reasons for the other person's distress. Then, choose from these solutions to defuse the anger:

- Say it like it is (But you know you could get fired for having meltdowns at work).
- Use humor (Wow! You can really explode—and that's an understatement!).
- Disarm; don't attack (How would you change the situation you're in if you could?).

- Save face (I'm going to keep this between us—I know it's been difficult for you.)
- Assure of acceptance (Many people here really like you).
- Express admiration (I've always admired the way you . . .).

After a minute or so of talking the other person down, reassuring him that he's likable or speaking positively about the angry person, his rage will usually subside. If the steps above are taken immediately after an initial outburst, an angry person is likely to contain anger better in the future.

Problem. "With so many people on special diets today, how far is a host expected to go in accommodating all the different requirements of guests?"

Solution. Most experts in entertaining etiquette agree that the host should make a "reasonable effort." That doesn't mean going as far as taking orders from every single guest before a party or holiday celebration. Making a reasonable effort can be accomplished by putting several choices on the buffet table.

a. If you plan to serve beef stroganoff with noodles, for example, and a few guests eat gluten-free, provide a side dish of rice.
b. If someone else is allergic to something in the sauce for beef stroganoff, cook a few portions of plain beef to offer as an alternative.

c. Provide two or three choices of vegetables in case someone can't digest corn or doesn't like spinach or asparagus.

The host shouldn't have to sacrifice the whole menu to please a few people. Another alternative is to ask guests to bring some of their own edible dishes to share. Good guests, who are just as important as good hosts when it comes to people-ability, should never bring all their own food and sit in a corner and eat it without sharing with others. That's not only insulting to the host, but it's extremely rude to other guests.

Problem. "I love taking my teenage daughter on business trips with me, but her manners need polishing. What should I say when she takes out her cell phone and starts texting someone while we're dining with my colleagues or business associates?"

Solution. To avoid an embarrassing confrontation in front of your associates, give your daughter the ground rules in advance. Explain to her that texting or talking on cell phones while dining with other people is only acceptable in emergencies. Tell her that doctors, for example, will excuse themselves before they pick up a call, even in cases of emergencies. Provide the consequences if she continues to ignore professional etiquette regarding electronic devices. Inform her that she'll have to leave her phone in the room the next time, or not come along on business trips at all if she doesn't follow the rules.

Problem. "What can I do to regain trust in a good friend who loaned me money that I couldn't pay back?"

Solution. The common-sense or obvious solution is to pay back the money, no matter how long it's been. Rather than make excuses why you couldn't come up with the cash sooner, simply apologize and ask to be reinstated as a friend. Remember the Rule of 10: You'll have to show responsibility at least 10 more times before complete trust is restored.

Problem. "So few retail representatives seem aware of good customer service today. How should I deal with store clerks who don't want to go out of their way to help me find what I need?"

Solution. If a clerk insists she can't do anything for you (without bothering to look for the product you need or suggest alternative choices), go to the customer service counter and complain. If there's no such counter, request to speak with a manager. A good store clerk will always at least try to find something or ask someone else on staff before letting a customer leave disgruntled.

Problem. "A former student asked me to help her find a job. Her work was always pretty good, but her appearance is sloppy and her people skills are poor. How can I help her without hurting her feelings?"

Solution. You may have to be honest. Being honest doesn't mean blurting out, "But you look like a mess and you can't get along with anyone." Be gentle. Ask a series of questions that might increase insight, self-awareness and job-seeking savvy:

- How do you dress when you go to interviews?
- Do you wash and style your hair?
- Do you smile, make eye contact and shake hands when introduced?
- What do you say about past supervisors—or fellow employees?

Questions like these open the door for further discussion, rather than hurt someone's feelings.

Problem. "I practice people skills all day with fellow workers, but when I get home it's hard to stay on course. I'm easily irritated by small things and show it. How can I extend my people-ability efforts to my family at the end of a long day at work?"

Solution: Because we're so closely tied and comfortable with one another, our families are often the last to receive the respect they deserve from us, especially when we're tired at the end of the day. Take a few moments to relax after you walk in the door, then doggedly pursue the practice of good people skills for the rest of the evening.

Problem. "The person in the cubicle next to me listens to the radio all day long, making it hard for me to concentrate on my work. How can I get her to turn it off without creating an office enemy?"

Solution. Tell the person that you can't concentrate on your work while listening to the radio. Suggest a win-win solution for both of you. Ask your co-worker to use earphones in the office so you can both work in the way that best suits you.

Good people skills save the day in many situations. People-ability takes you further in life than lack of it ever will. It's worth your time and effort to learn and practice interpersonal skills. Applying good people skills pays off in reaching career goals, making friends, building networks—and in countless other ways. Keep trying.

Edwards Brothers Malloy
Thorofare, NJ USA
April 13, 2012